MODERN-DAY PSALMS

MODERN-DAY PSALMS

Praise Songs and Love Messages

RICHARD. VINCENT. ROSE.

iUniverse LLC
Bloomington

MODERN-DAY PSALMS
PRAISE SONGS AND LOVE MESSAGES

iUniverse books may be ordered through booksellers or by contacting:

iUniverse LLC
1663 Liberty Drive
Bloomington, IN 47403
www.iuniverse.com
1-800-Authors (1-800-288-4677)

Because of the dynamic nature of the Internet, any web addresses or links contained in this book may have changed since publication and may no longer be valid. The views expressed in this work are solely those of the author and do not necessarily reflect the views of the publisher, and the publisher hereby disclaims any responsibility for them.

Any people depicted in stock imagery provided by Thinkstock are models, and such images are being used for illustrative purposes only.
Certain stock imagery © Thinkstock.

ISBN: 978-1-4917-1203-0 (sc)
ISBN: 978-1-4917-1204-7 (hc)
ISBN: 978-1-4917-1205-4 (e)

Library of Congress Control Number: 2013919013

Printed in the United States of America.

iUniverse rev. date: 11/13/2013

Contents

PART II

PART III

Introduction

For several years, I have had the distinct privilege and honor to be allowed to share many of my poems, works, and thoughts with dear friends all over the world. God has been so good to me, and has proven Himself faithful in every way.

This is the first opportunity to put many of the favorites, most requested, and new works, into a single volume. My prayer is that you will be encouraged, inspired, edified, comforted, and blessed as you read, and allow your very soul to absorb the words.

I have said so many times that I am not the writer; I just operated the pen, as God spoke through the writing instrument. Many of these works I wrote in just a few minutes, the words being given to me as fast as I could write them. Some have taken over ten years to complete. As with any writer, how often I have been awakened in the middle of the night, as God speaks to me, giving me a new idea. Just as often, just before I fall asleep, I have to go running down the hallway, into the office, to write something new, or to add to something I am working on. I try to always carry a pen and paper "on me," where ever I go. I have written on bank envelopes, restaurant napkins, brown paper shopping bags, and even on airline "sick bags." Without a writing surface, I've written on the hood of a car, on someone's back, on windows and walls, and on picnic tables. I never know where I'll be when God gives me something new. The important thing is that I am always listening. It is important to me for you to be able to "feel" the words, touching your very heart and soul. Often, I have read the words over the telephone, even to a non-believing audience, and been told, "I can't explain it, but I have this funny feeling deep down . . . I can feel something I've never felt before . . ."

I can say, without doubt, that God is still inspiring writing, and writers, today. I know where my writing comes from, the Source of my writing inspiration. I feel that the greatest writing gift God has given me is the ability to make someone laugh and cry in the same work. God will use whatever means necessary to reach out to us. He can even use me. And, you. At the heart of my message to young writers, or artists of any type, to whom God has given a particular gift, is to use it. The tragedy, what so often happens, is that we are so busy with "life," that we are too "busy" to do the work which God has given us the very gift for. We all have gifts, every one of us, which God wants to use. All of us. Even you.

There are three distinct times when God gives you something specific to write. One is when you are dealing with something which has happened to you, something which brings joy, or heartbreak-either of which can be called indescribable. God gives you something just for you, to help you understand, and just "get through" that time.
You then realize that what God has given you, can also help others to understand, and "get through" their time of great trial. The second time is when you are called upon, in a particular situation, to write something special, for a specific situation. The third time, which, to me, is perhaps the most awe-inspiring, is when God gives you something completely "out of the blue." When you have a close relationship with God, this means that you are speaking with Him all of the time, and He is speaking to you. You are both listening. And, responding. You realize that, regardless of the situation, God has not given the message just to you, or just for you. It is for everyone who has gone through that particular situation in the past, is going through it now, or will go through it in the future. The key is "through it." God, and only God, can get you through those situations. A constant theme of my writing is that God gets you through, so that you can then "go back in" and help other people out. I am constantly reminded that the first word in "gospel" is "go." In order for you to know the way out, you would have had to have "been there" first.

I can't stress enough, that another constant theme of my writing, is that what I thought was the worst thing that ever happened to me, turned out to be the best thing that ever happened to me.

Modern-Day Psalms? Praise Songs? Love Messages? Many of the love songs and poems I've included are metaphoric in nature, describing the love Christ has for us, and the love we have for Him. He is the lover of our souls, and the greatest joy a human can experience is an intimate relationship with Him. We are, after all, His bride. We are to love our wives just as He loves the church. So, I do not shrink away from saying that it's ok to love your wife, and, to love Jesus . . . both . . . with all your heart and soul.

While the individual works included in this volume have a true purpose, it is also the introductions to the works, and the stories behind the works, which God has wanted me to share. I have included a brief, or at least as brief as I could make it, introduction to each of the poems and songs in this volume. It has been my experience that it can be as much of an encouragement, help, and a blessing to know the story behind a particular work, as the work itself. For that reason, I have shared thoughts, part of the "messages" which God intended for this volume to be, at the beginning of each individual work. Some will be blessed and encouraged by the works, some by the introductions, and some by both. It is all part of His plan for this volume.

After Part I, I have included the actual stories behind some of the works, and some additional messages which go along with some of the individual works.

I'd like to mention that this is not a "self-help" book, but a "His-Help" book, because I can't do it on my own. Nor, can you. I need God's help every day, in every way. I need His help to think the right way, to act the right way, and to write and speak the right words. I understand that the world says, "One day at a time," and I can respect and appreciate that. However, Christians know that we need God's help every moment of every day. Sometimes, we have to take it one hour, one minute, and even one second at a time. I need God's help with every step I take, and every word I write and speak.

I am often asked about the unique spelling and punctuation of my name, especially the periods after each individual name. Here is the explanation:

My pen name is a combination of names, meant to honor both my parents, and my wife's parents. My father's name is Richard; Carol's father's name is Vincent, and her mother's name is Rose. When I explain this, I always get the obvious question:

"OK, I understand about your father's name, and Carol's parents' names. But, you said your name honors all four parents. What about your mother?"

Well, actually, my mother's name is included three times . . . You see, my mother's name is Dorothy . . . You know what everyone calls her? "Dot."

You may also notice that I use a lot of what I call "3 dots" (. . .) in my writing. I know that "officially" this is called an ellipsis . . . but, I call it "3 dots." One of the rarely used definitions for using an ellipsis is for a pause . . . to reflect. I certainly hope my writing makes you think and reflect on subjects that have the deepest meanings for you. I don't know of any other writer who uses the "dots" as often as I do. Editors hate it . . . but . . . this is just another way, interspersed throughout my writing . . . that I honor my Mom . . . and, all Moms. In addition, many of the poems are specifically written to be read in public, during a service or ceremony, so there are times when the "pause" is built-in.

You will also notice that I capitalize personal pronouns which relate to Jesus, and to God. It is considered proper to *not capitalize* "He" or "You" when referring to deity, in written form. The explanation given is that, even in Scripture, the capitalization is not used. I always use the capital letters when I write, as a way to honor Them.

I also always capitalize the word "Pastor." I know that when we use the word "President" in front of a President's name, we always capitalize it. I have corresponded with both Presidents and Pastors, and I will always capitalize both. However . . . "*The office of Pastor is the greatest office in the land. For, the people choose the President. God chooses the Pastor.*"

I have also been asked why, in putting together a volume of my works, I did not include illustrations to go with the works. I am blessed to have friends who are artists and illustrators. However, since the very beginning, God made me realize that it is not about the pictures, or the illustrations. It's all about the words. And, as I was compiling this volume, God clearly reminded me of that. It will always be about the words. God's words moving though a mind, heart, and soul, through a writing instrument, and onto paper.

To be read. To touch the reader's mind, heart, and soul. We all have our own pictures to go with the words, just as the words speak to us individually.

Please enjoy this volume, and be blessed by the real messages behind the works. God has been gracious to allow me the privilege to write words to honor so many of those, in our daily lives, who are deserving of our love, respect, and our honor.

It is not the job which gives honor to the man.
It is the man which gives honor to the job.

Blessings to each of you,
Richard. Vincent. Rose.

P.S. Genesis 12:3
    Hebrews 6:15

P.S.S: Pray More.
      + Study More.
      = Be More (Like Jesus).

Dedication

Please allow me to dedicate this volume to my Lord and Savior, Jesus Christ, my wife Carol (besides salvation, the greatest gift God has ever given me), and to my family.

I had a long, hard struggle with the time it took to complete my Biblical studies, and obtain my Degree in Theology. Here is a promise I made to my Assistant Pastor, very early on in the process: "I will get my degree. And, when I walk up to the podium to receive the degree, I won't be alone. No, all three of us will walk up, together: Me in the middle, Jesus on one side, and Carol on the other side."

During personal speaking engagements, I try to always open with this:
"First, I'd like to say that I love Jesus.
I think we need more men who will stand up and say, 'I love Jesus.'
I love my wife.
I think we need more men who will stand up and say, 'I love my wife.'
I love my family.
I think we need more men who will stand up and say, 'I love my family.'"

Blessings to you, and your family,
R.V.R.

Acceptance
INTRODUCTION

Whether by accident, illness, or military casualty, to have one's child taken, by any means, is the most difficult tragedy of all to face. However, it seems so much harder to accept when it is an infant or a young child, meaning also that the parents will be very young, and often, this is the first real tragedy of their lives that they've had to face.

"Acceptance" was written as a result of the loss of an infant, who never left the hospital. She never arrived home, where a nursery had been lovingly prepared by her two overjoyed parents.

While I was grieving for their child, God gave me this poem. I wrote it, in one sitting, early one morning, while sitting in my van, in our driveway. For the first time, I couldn't think of a title for a poem. I think it was because I was still in shock over the child's death, and "Why?" I struggled with the question of the title for several days. A few days later, Carol and I were staying on Cape Cod, a weekend getaway. I still hadn't come up with a title, even though I couldn't stop thinking about it. This had just never happened before.

In the middle of the night, I was abruptly awakened . . . God spoke to me, clearly and plainly, and He only spoke one word: "Acceptance."

It is the only time I have ever written a poem, in which the title is not included within the body of the work.

Acceptance

Even though I never knew you
I won't forget you
Even though I never knew you
I loved you
Even though I never knew you
I'll miss you

Even though you left so soon
I won't forget that you were here
Even though you are gone
I'll still hold you near

All at once you were our little girl
All at once you became Heaven's pearl
Did the angels create such a fuss
That you would have to suddenly leave us?
To go, help prepare a place
Tidy up a bit
To help make ready a place
Where so much love could fit

As my loving parents
You went before
But now, as your loving child
I've gone ahead to stand at Heaven's door

For, I have gone to prepare a place
In the very presence of God's grace
Now, I wait for you to join me
The first glimpse *of you* I am waiting to see

How big? How tall?
The color of your hair
Will you have any hair at all?
I don't care how you look
It doesn't matter, you see
For I love you
And want to spend all my time with thee

RICHARD. VINCENT. ROSE.

I'll have so much to show you
There'll be so much to learn
But, I'll place you under my wing
And, in just a moment
You will know everything

The answers to questions
You've always had
How life can sometimes be so sad
How something called life
Can even contain death
And, Why? Why? Why?
Elizabeth?

Some answers you will only learn here
That is why this place
You should hold so dear
To get *here*, to see me
Should be your career

To get here, on your list, should be first
Believe me, there are places worse
For it is here that I stand waiting for you
My cheeks are still chubby, my eyes are still blue
The only thing missing is both of you

You must accept that the reason I'm here
You may never know
But somehow, not knowing
Will, it must, make your faith grow
For, faith is believing in what you can't see
Even if what you can't see . . . is me

So, hold to your faith
And accept what must be
And believe that one day
Once again, you'll be holding me

A Dictionary, a Primer, and a Blue Back Speller
INTRODUCTION

Many of the articles and features I've done contain at least a parting reference to how, here in the United States, "times have changed," or "it doesn't seem like that long ago."

I wanted to write something to honor three of the great textbooks/ reference books used in the early history of the United States.

Noah Webster's 1828 Dictionary, _An American Dictionary of the English Language_, was the first American dictionary published, written by the man called "The Father of American Christian Education." Noah Webster used the Bible as the foundation for his definitions, and the writing was consistent with the documents and books written during that time.

David Barton's 1777 _New England Primer_ was the first textbook ever printed in America, and was used to teach reading and Bible lessons in our schools until the twentieth century. It has been called "The single most influential Christian textbook in history." It was first published in 1690.

Noah Webster's Blue Back Speller, titled _A Grammatical Institute of the English Language_, was published in 1783. "Old Blue Back" provided a Christ-centered approach to teaching children.

These textbooks proved that moral truths could be taught in every school subject.

A Dictionary, a Primer, and a Blue Back Speller

Oh, that I could turn back the hands of time!
Before the penny was wheat
And the stores were not dime
The money was silver
Or even gold
When we ruled the world
Or, so I am told

I read of a time
When the New England Primer
Noah Webster's 1828 Dictionary
And the Blue Back Speller
Were the textbooks of choice
It seemed the whole world
Loved and admired us
And, in our freedom, did rejoice

Was it really that many years back?
Nestled firmly away in Father Time's sack

A dictionary, a primer, an old blue book
Paired with the Bible and prayer
A great nation educated and forged
We must go back, to return there

I remember, and have read of a time
When our nation was so great
Founded in faith
Let's return before it's too late

In God we trust
Was on every coin
We stood alone, independent
Organizations we didn't need to join

When we trusted in God
We were kings of the world
Nations would stand in respect
When our flag was unfurled

God is still God
Jesus is still King
When did we start to think
That we ruled everything?
Our nation used to get down on her knees
Now, we kneel to every sin and disease

God puts them down
And sets others up
Nations are His agents
Sometimes made to drink from a bitter cup

If we turn back to God
Just like how we'd begun
We would again rule the world
Just like our Father's only Son

Our future can be bright
Once again
If we'll just turn from sin
And turn back to Him

Our founding fathers were not perfect
And neither am I
But what they used
I am willing to try

Yes, I want to be proud of our nation again
I also need to set aside every sin
My own foundation needs to ring true
Like my fathers before me
I need to trust only you

A Bible with textbook
I need to have on my shelf
I need to serve others
And not just myself

To my nation's original creed
I must be true
But, to do that
I'll have to turn back to you

Let's return to a time
When we were the greatest of great
There is still time
But, let's return before it's too late

Airborne
INTRODUCTION

This is the poem which I wrote on board an airplane, somewhere between Atlanta, GA, and Newport News, Virginia.

Once again, I had not followed my own advice, meaning that I had no paper when the poem came to me. At least I had the ever-present pen. Looking around, or more realistically, looking in front of my knees, at the pouch on the back of the seat in front of me, I searched for something to write on.

Airline magazines, shopping mall, but no paper. Then . . . what's this? White paper! Someone must have left some pages from a notepad, or the airline had thought to supply writing paper for its passengers. As I pulled out the paper, I realized it wasn't from a notebook. In fact, it wasn't writing paper at all . . . It was some sort of paper bag, with a slick, lined interior . . . Then, I realized what the bag was . . . I looked around to make sure no one was watching, and then applied pen to bag, and the ink took! I looked around again, making sure no one had noticed . . . However, you should have seen the look on the person, sitting next to me, when, after I had "filled" both sides of the bag with poetry . . . I asked him if I could please use his bag . . .

I was so grateful that God had given me my partner for life. Don't worry: I checked, and I honestly can't find anywhere in Scripture where it's not ok to love your wife. In fact, we are supposed to love them! We are supposed to be deeply in love with them! It's even ok to show them that you love them! It's even ok to write them a love letter, or poem!

Enjoy the feeling of being "Airborne."

Airborne

All the faces look the same
As I hurriedly board the plane
I wonder, as we get ready to split the clouds above
I can't help but think, "Is anyone else so much in love?"

The feeling in my stomach
As we lift off the ground
Still not as thrilling
As this love that I've found

You are all I can think about
As my plane gets aloft
Your eyes, your lips
Your skin, so soft

Row 16 on the 3-seat side
I buckle up and prepare for the ride
10,000 feet, when the clouds we break through
Still, all I can think of is you

Flight attendants breeze by asking
"Is there anything I can get?"
I think, "No, thank you, all I need
Is at home, in Connecticut"

The sound of your voice
Lifts me higher than any jet
The way you hold me so tight
Something I just can't forget

For, when you said yes
On that fate-filled night
It was then that my whole, entire life
Took flight

20,000 feet and the sky is so blue
Still . . . nothing as beautiful as you

God is so wonderful
To give you to me
To serve Him, to love you
Is the best life can be

The landscape below
As I peer over the wing
I hear the way that you danced
And started to sing

The engine hums loudly
I'm lulled to sleep by the view
If I hurry and nap, maybe, just maybe
I'll dream about you

33,000 feet
Smooth as the morning dove
Not fear of flying
Fear of being in love

But, you changed all that
And brought me around
In the game of life
Super Bowl won! Winning touchdown!

Below, all white cotton
Above, all clear skies
Still not as pretty
As the look in your eyes

We tilt to the left
We tilt to the right
Still not as airborne
As I was that night

Four miles up
I'm still in love with you
Counting the days until
We both say "I do"

I look out my window
And stare into space
And yet, all I can see
Is the love on your face

Lakes and rivers
Look like puddles and streams
37,000 feet brought me
The girl of my dreams

Highways and roads
Look like x's and o's
I start at your head
And end at your toes

The whole world looks like golf courses
As we turn to land
The gold in your heart as pure
As your wedding band

Seat belt sign on
As I buckle back in
I'm thinking as we kiss the ground
"When will I kiss you again?"

The lady behind me says "Jesus" and "Thank you, God"
As she claps her hands
My words exactly, and I'm so thankful
That God heard my prayers, and that He understands

Amazing Grace: The Jesus Amendments
INTRODUCTION

Two years after completing _Amazing Grace-The John Newton Story_, God laid it on my heart to write a brand new verse to "Amazing Grace." So I tried, and I tried, to write something "good" that would fit, but I couldn't find the right words. Then, God showed me that John Newton did not "make up" the song; he wrote it from his own personal experience.

Like so many of us, I have been knocked completely off my feet, stunned beyond imagination by betrayal, tragedy, and personal loss. Knocked down . . . face down . . . not having the strength or will-power to even make it back up to my knees. When friends or family fall into sin and desert us, it is Jesus' hand that reaches down, and lifts us up . . . I don't mean up to the top of the mountain, or up to a pedestal . . . it's Jesus' hand that reaches down, and lifts us up . . . to our knees.

I ended up writing three new verses to "Amazing Grace."

Put simply, these three new verses glorify and honor Jesus.
The first verse tells us what Jesus does, the second verse tells us who Jesus is, and the last verse just lifts up His holy name.

Amazing Grace: The Jesus Amendments
(Traditional Melody)

Though friends and fam'ly 'round me fall
Stricken by sin's disease
It's Jesus' hand that reaches down
And lifts me to my knees

Jesus, Savior, is Lord of Lords
Jesus, the King of Kings
Jesus, the Prince of Peace is Lord
And God of Every Thing

Jesus, Jesus, Jesus, Jesus
Jesus, Jesus, Jesus
Jesus, Jesus, Jesus, Jesus
Jesus, Jesus, Jesus

Amazing Grace: All Known Verses
INTRODUCTION

God's "Amazing Grace."

Perhaps, next to the 23rd Psalm, there is no other song ever written that is used so widely to bring comfort and peace to troubled souls. Even the tune, without words, brings the same relief and consolation.

Time and again, our forefathers publicly acknowledged that it was God's grace that gave us our country, our liberty, and our freedom. From Washington to Adams to Lincoln, and almost every leader between or since, it has been recognized that it is only God's grace that will allow us to keep it.
Today, the only true source of our healing, the only real hope we have is through the exact same source. These men knew that true greatness, for an individual or for a nation, begins from the knees. It is the measure, the allotment, and the sheer endurance of His grace that is amazing.

We are going to present all known existing verses of the song, "Amazing Grace."

For our historians: Note that when John Newton wrote the first six verses, the song was not entitled "Amazing Grace." And, another verse, verse seven, known as the "10,000 years" verse, was added by an unknown author, and first appeared as early as 1829, in a hymnal that was published by a Mr. R. Winchell, from Wethersfield, CT.
So, adding another verse to "Amazing Grace" has already been done, and accepted. It is an "amazing" coincidence that now, 184 years later, a new verse has been written and added to the original . . . also written, and first appearing, in Connecticut.

Now, for the first time ever published, here are the known verses to "Amazing Grace," with "Amazing Grace: The Jesus Amendments" included. We started with the "Praise God" and "I'm Saved" choruses, as these are such widely accepted additions to the song, in many churches today. Please enjoy!

Amazing Grace: All Known Verses

Praise God! Praise God! Praise God! Praise God!
Praise God! Praise God! Praise God!
Praise God! Praise God! Praise God! Praise God!
Praise God! Praise God! Praise God!

I'm saved! I'm saved! I'm saved! I'm saved!
I'm saved! I'm saved! I'm saved!
I'm saved! I'm saved! I'm saved! I'm saved!
I'm saved! I'm saved! I'm saved!

Amazing grace! How Sweet the sound
That saved a wretch like me!
I once was lost, but now am found
Was blind, but now I see

'Twas grace that taught my heart to fear
And grace my fears relieved
How precious did that grace appear
The hour I first believed

Through many dangers, toils, and snares
I have already come
'Tis grace hath brought me safe thus far
And grace will lead me home

The Lord has promised good to me
His Word my hope secures
He will my Shield and Portion be
As long as life endures

Yea, when this flesh and heart shall fail
And mortal life shall cease
I shall possess, within the veil
A life of joy and peace

The earth shall soon dissolve like snow
The sun forbear to shine
But God, who called me here below
Shall be forever mine

When we've been there ten thousand years
Bright shining as the sun
We've no less days to sing God's praise
Than when we'd first begun

Though friends and fam'ly 'round me fall
Stricken by sin's disease
It's Jesus' hand that reaches down
And lifts me to my knees

Jesus, Savior, is Lord of Lords
Jesus, the King of Kings
Jesus, the Prince of Peace is Lord
And God of Every Thing

Jesus, Jesus, Jesus, Jesus
Jesus, Jesus, Jesus
Jesus, Jesus, Jesus, Jesus
Jesus, Jesus, Jesus

A Vision from the Lord
INTRODUCTION

I began to write this while I was caught up in the Spirit, during a worship service at a church in Carrollton, GA. At that time, the church had blank "Sermon Notes" sheets, which were kept on a table at the rear of the church. From what I can tell from the sheet, as this was the only "sermon note" I had written, the sermon must have had the title, or at least the line, "Revelation or Information?" Those are the only three words pertaining to the sermon I had written, so if the Pastor reads this, well, allow me to say it was a great sermon! It must have been, for, somehow, in the midst of the meeting, I was carried away for a glimpse of Heaven. The rest of the sheet, front and back, was filled out, completely with words describing this "vision."

I must confess that, often, I get great inspiration while sitting in church, and the inspiration can come at any time. Some of my best writing has been done on the back of a Church Bulletin, on the "Notes from Sermon" lines. I can't be the only one, can I? Maybe the Pastor would forgive me, because, after all, his preaching was good enough to send me all the way to Heaven!

A Vision from the Lord

One night, while in my prayer closet
I had a vision from the Lord
I was taken away; I knew not where
But, through the heavens I soared

On angel's wings I was carried
To a land far away
Where I saw no sun overhead
But the light was as the middle of the day

I felt just so peaceful
There was such calm in the air
What I saw with my eyes
Visions of grandeur cannot compare

Then a voice broke the silence with
"Be not afraid. Good tidings I bring."
I'm sure in the distance
I heard angels sing

But how could I know?
I'd not heard angels before
It was then, there, just ahead
I saw someone standing by a door

Not a regular door
This was immense
And, was that the smell?
The smell of incense?

Then, the door opened
I feared I might lose my sight
For never before have I beheld, what I can only describe
As a pure, blinding light

As I squinted through the cracks
My fingers covering my face
I thought, "How can I be here?
In such a place?"

Then, I saw this messenger, this angel, whatever he was
Standing before me, arrayed in white clothes
As he stood by the doorway
I saw his right arm, as it arose

"He will see you now," he said
In a voice so calm, so solemn, so right
Then, he just walked off
Into the light

There was something about the way he said "He"
That sent a chill through my soul
Yet, for reasons I can't explain
I felt such peace, and joy, I could not control

But, all the while, I kept on thinking,
"There must be some mistake.
There had to be someone else
That they were supposed to take."

Then, all at once
A presence came over me
When I lifted my eyes
In a strange way, I was able to see

I could now see through the light
And it was then I discovered I was not alone
For, off in the distance, yet as clear as the day
I saw it-the Throne

The Throne, yes the Throne
This just cannot be! This cannot be happening to me!
If that is the Throne, then that means to my left
That is where Jesus would be
I must have passed out
But when I awoke
Over my eyes
There was some kind of a cloak

It was then that I saw
The real mercy seat
And that's when I found out
I had been brought to His feet

The first thing I thought
"I'm not worthy to look upon His face."
Then, the next thought I had
Was about mercy, and grace

And then, I heard it! I heard it!
The voice of Jesus, as He said,
"My child, I am so glad you could come."
My soul was so filled with His glory
Just from His words
I was struck dumb

He called me His child
I fell before Him, on my face
And again, all I could think of
Was His love, His mercy, and His grace

From that moment on
He spoke to my heart
His words so powerful
My body, my soul, rose with a start

I could not comprehend
Why, for me, He would send

"My Lord, I am not worthy to stand here.
You must have sent for someone else; someone who is now overdue.
Surely it was not me that you sent for."
"Yes, my child, it was you."

"But, Lord, I am a sinner!"
"You were, yes, before you met me.
Now, you are a saint, and in my eyes,
And, my Father's, forever will be."

"Did you not accept me, trust me, as your Lord and Savior,
And confess me before men?
And, if you go back,
Will you still trust me, and confess me, again?"

"Yes, Lord
I did accept you as my Lord and Savior,
And confess you before men.
I was just afraid
That you would not accept me
Because of my sin."

"Jesus, you have done so much for me
And I feel that I have done nothing for you.
So often, in my life, sin did abound.
Time after time,
You picked me up
It seems like all I've done is let you down."

Then, the sound of His voice
Made the whole earth shake
"I have a bride
That I will be coming back to take.
What a day that will be.
Just be ready, be ready for me.

This time, you came to me.
Next time, I'll be coming to you.
And, if you go back,
Will you still trust, and confess me, too?"

I now have before me a race, a race to be won
I live with this vision, which helps me to run
And, I live for that day,
When I hear His voice saying,
"Well done."

By This Time Next Year
INTRODUCTION

We've all been there. All of us, including me, more times than we wished: At the bedside of a loved one, during their final hours. The sounds, and the silence, in the days leading up to the end, when it seems all we are doing, all we can be doing . . . is waiting . . . waiting . . . for the doctor's report.

I wanted to write something from the standpoint of the person who was dying, and who knew that the end was near. Someone who had great faith and trust in where they were going. Someone who had strong enough faith to dry *our* tears; to cheer *us* up. God gave me this.

Like many of the works which God gives me, the underlying emphasis is not on now . . . but later . . . for us. To encourage us to make the right choices now, to ensure that we will get there, too. They know where they are going, they know in whom they have believed, and they are even excited to get there! The only evident worry they have is whether we'll make the right choice, so that we can join them later.

By This Time Next Year

She was but a child
So weak and so frail
For months, we'd been praying
But, she just wouldn't get well

The doctors had done all they could do
The nurses had given all they could give
It was time for the family meeting
She would have just six months to live

Or, maybe nine months
A year, who knows?
It may all depend
On the treatment we chose

We listened in silence
As the doctor spoke
When all of a sudden
The silence broke

From her sick bed, she lovingly looked around the room
She smiled at each of us, and looked almost glad
Why, oh why, her voice breaking the gloom,
Does everyone look so sad?

By this time next year
I'll be walking on streets of gold
I'll be walking with Jesus
As eternity unfolds

There will be no more dying
No sickness, no sin
No more doctors
No more nurses, or syringe

There will be no more wheelchairs
Or walkers or canes
I'll be shouting for glory
Around the throne with the saints

By this time next year
I'll be walking on streets of gold
Gone to a land
Where we'll never grow old
Walking with Jesus
Don't worry about me
I've got something to look forward to
Can't you see?

By this time next year
I'll be able to run
Now, why would you want me
To miss out on that fun?

I consider myself blessed
So, don't spend any more time grieving
I have an advantage
Because I know when I'm leaving

I can't wait to see Jesus!
I'm looking ahead
I'm really excited
I'll never have to get back into bed!

By this time next year
Oh, why can't you see?
All things will be passed away
All things, that is, but me

I can't wait to see my Savior and Lord
To walk, and to walk, and to walk some more
No, I don't think I'll even sit down
Except, of course, to adjust my crown

I know where I'm going
What if you knew?
Would you feel the same way
If this happened to you?

By this time next year
I know where I'll be
My only concern is
Will you be there with me?

Connecticut-Land of My Love
INTRODUCTION

I went through a phase (you're never too old, right?) where I wanted to write a special poem for each state in the United States. Each state I have visited has touched me in different ways. Just like people, God made them all different, yet beautiful, with enduring and appealing qualities. I considered doing a whole "State Songs" collection. I started with Connecticut, and now, years later, I am still at "Connecticut" in the state column, but, who knows? Maybe one day . . .

After all, I love every state. And, the more I travel, the more I see to love. Even traveling to other countries, I see beauty in what God has made, for everyone to enjoy. God made the planet, and just like states, each country reflects His creation, and His creativity. I think He's done a great job!

This started out as a love song for Carol, and then, it became a love song for the state. I battled with, "Can you love Connecticut (or any state), if you aren't from there? If you weren't born and raised there?" Well, I fell in love with Carol, and I had never seen her before.

We haven't lived there for many years, but, as Carol's home state, and after my experiences there, I still love "The Constitution State."

Connecticut-Land of My Love

Connecticut
Land of my love
Connecticut
Blue skies above

Flowing brooks and mountain streams
Connecticut
You hold my dreams

Stars so bright
Grass so green
A meadow soft
A winter scene

Just like me
She changes from year to year
You never know when
Her beauty will appear

We trample long through
The ice and the snow
What tomorrow brings
We never know

Rhododendrons and laurel
The flowers of spring
When the frost is all gone
It's not just the birds that will sing

Connecticut
Land of my love
Never seen such gorgeous days
Never seen such blue skies above

Connecticut
Where the seasons follow you
Where ever you may go
Connecticut
Your touch falls as gently
As the first falling snow

So complete
She's got it all
Three months each
Of winter, spring, summer, and fall

Connecticut
I just can't leave her
Connecticut
Loved her since first I'd seen her

Connecticut
Land of my love

Deal!
INTRODUCTION

Here's another example of using the Church Bulletin "Sermon Notes" in place of my own paper.

I just never know when God will give me something brand new, and I must always be ready to write.

Come to think of it . . . I think the church even supplied the pen! However, if I wasn't there, in person, listening, I would have never received this idea.

Here, Jesus and Satan are engaged in a card game. Satan is the dealer, thinking he holds all of the cards. They may be scarred, but Jesus still has the winning hands!

Deal!

Often, the game of life has been compared to a card game, or a deck of cards has been used to explain life. Let's imagine that both examples are real:

Satan, standing, would be the dealer.
Jesus, sitting alone, would be the player.

Satan deals: The card is "Sin."
Jesus responds, "I can beat that."

Satan deals: The card is "Sickness."
Jesus responds, "I can beat that."

Satan deals: The card is "Disease."
Jesus responds, "I can beat that."

Card after card is dealt, each card revealing a fact of human life, the human condition.
Each time, Jesus responds in exactly the same way:
"I can beat that."

Running out of cards, Satan hastily deals the rest of his cards, which he greedily holds:
Satan deals: The card is "Death."
Jesus responds, "I can beat that."

Satan, now sweating, deals: The card is "Hell."
Jesus responds, "I can beat that."

Satan, now confident, and eerily smiling,
Deals: The card is "The Grave."
Jesus responds, "I can beat that."

The scene now moves from the card table, to just outside a tomb, which is open:

Jesus, now standing, slowly, and deliberately, steps out of the tomb. He pauses, leans on a huge rock, and looks back at what is now an empty tomb, and calmly responds:
"I can beat that."

Now, looking straight ahead, through time . . . looking directly at the dealer,
Jesus responds:
"Game Over."

Dear God, I Just Don't Understand
INTRODUCTION

This was born out of the most difficult of circumstances, loneliness, and, honestly, a strong dose of self-pity. Let's be honest: In our heart of hearts, we can feel like we are God's favorite, a chosen vessel, a "special case" in everything we do. This feeling of self-worth and value can be even greater when we are devoting our time and efforts to the ministry. We are working for Him, right? So, don't we deserve, yes *deserve* special treatment?

I had suffered the worst type of betrayal, I was all alone, forced to move into a new place to live, and I was traveling, living in hotels, at least five days a week. Just when I thought I was "coming out of it," I injured my right leg, and could not walk. For weeks, I couldn't walk unassisted, and didn't know if I'd ever be able to run again. Just after my ankle injury had healed, I endured two separate dog attacks in one day, re-injuring my right leg, and mangling my left leg. It seemed every day, I was alone, crippled, emotionally torn apart, and,

"Dear God, I just didn't understand."

Dear God, I Just Don't Understand

Dear God
I just don't understand
I thought that I was
Your main man
Yet, here I am
Crippled, hurt
Unable to stand

Dear God
I just don't know
What you have in mind
I just don't know
Which way
The road will unwind
Dear God
Please God
Tell me
If you don't mind

I know I must have fallen
Out of your will
But I just want you to know
That I love you still
And will love you
Even if I have to start
Getting my clothes from Goodwill

Dear God
I'm sorry
And I want you to
Please take me back
I know that you
Won't put me back on the rack
Because I am healed
By the stripes on your back

Dear God
I love you God
I need you God
I need you
In Jesus' name I pray
I need you God
I need you
Every single day

I need you God
In every way
For I know
That without you beside me
I realize that
I am such easy prey

Dear God
There is one thing
That I do understand
To take one step
I need to hold
To your unchanging hand
For only then
Can I get back up
Not only to walk
But most of all
Stand

Don't Weep For Me
INTRODUCTION

Next to "Why, Pastor, Why," the memorial poem "Don't Weep for Me" is perhaps the work most associated with my writing. It was written especially for the memorial service for my father-in-law, Vincent Martone, and was actually written on the day which Mr. Martone passed away. Mr. Martone was a war veteran, and I included this, as well as some phrases he was known for, within the body of the work.

I have had the honor of reading "Don't Weep for Me" at many services, and have given the poem to close friends, to help and comfort them during times of great mourning.
Much as with "Why, Pastor, Why," I realized that "Don't Weep for Me" was not given for just one person, or for one memorial service. It was given to comfort and encourage all those in our Christian family who have suffered grief and sorrow as a result of losing loved ones.

I pray that you'll be comforted by the words, and that you realize the great hope and comfort we have in times of our greatest sadness. Know that only Jesus can truly comfort us; only He can give us real peace in these times of sorrow.

Don't Weep For Me
Original Version

Don't weep for me
If you could see
What I now see
You would not weep . . . you would shout "Victory!"

I know that only sadness now you feel
But, you need to know that Heaven is real
If you could only see the streets of gold, the pearly gate
You would not cry, you might even envy my fate

The skies are always sunny, bathed in God's own light
There is no more rain, no clouds, and no more night
I've left behind sickness, heartache, and pain
No more tears, broken dreams; for now, all is gain

For, here, there is no more sorrow, poverty, or lack
I can tell you now-I don't ever want to go back
Back to the earth, and the trials every day . . .
No, I'll take Jesus, and peace . . . right here I will stay

Don't weep for me now
You don't know what you do!
Don't wish I was there
For if you only knew!

On November 4th, at 3:25
It was not that I died, I became alive
I have no more sickness, no more pain
There will be no more clouds, no thunder, no rain

I served my country in Europe, in lands across the sea
But it is only now that I've seen real victory
I've traveled from the battlefield to serve Uncle Sam
And now I've landed safely in the bosom of Abraham

For, here in eternity I will forever rest
And walk down these streets with the one called "Blessed"
For I have reached my eternal reward
With the chorus of saints I join in one accord

I don't have time now to shed just one tear
I can only hope that one day, you too, will be here
My body I've left, but why should you grieve?
I've traded it all for this new body I've received

I'm singing right now, and laughing out loud
If you could see me right now, I know you'd be proud
I trusted in Jesus, and Jesus alone
I traded my hospital bed to sit on God's throne

There should be only one reason for you all to cry
And that is to not know where you'll go when you die
For one day you'll die and you'll be right here
But, if you've trusted in Jesus, you'll have nothing to fear

I'll wait, and I'll wait for you to decide
If you don't trust Jesus, then I'll be the one who cried

So, don't weep for me
You know the gospel is true
Follow its course
Lest, from above, I weep for you

So, just remember, if you start to cry
Instead, just look up at that big, blue sky
I'm looking down to tell you again, just like days gone by,
That "God loves you . . . and . . . so do I . . ."

Don't Weep For Me (Mama Version)
INTRODUCTION

When I read "Don't Weep for Me" at a memorial service, I always change the paragraph about military service, to fit the life of the one to whom the service is being given for, always leaving the "bosom of Abraham" reference to close that personalized paragraph.

When my beloved Mother went to be with Jesus, it was early on Valentine's Day . . . February 14, 2013. During the period of mourning that followed, I wanted to re-write "Don't Weep for Me" in honor of Mama.

I went in and added words that detailed what she most loved in her life: Jesus, and her family. Mama loved the Psalms; it was her favorite book. I also could not leave out the fact that, when Jesus came and got her, it was Valentine's Day.

Something else about Valentine's Day: February 14th is also my mother-in-law's birthday, who passed away on Good Friday, in 2003. Let's just say that neither of those days will ever be the same again.

Please allow me to comfort and encourage you with these words: As a parent, when it comes to your children, there are three things you most worry about when they are away from the house, gone with friends, etc. These would be:

1. Where they are.
2. Who they are with.
3. When will you see them again?

Now, as a loving son . . . when Mama left us . . . so much of the pain and agony was taken away, because:

1. I knew where she was.
2. I knew who she was with.
3. I knew that I would see her again.

Don't Weep For Me
Mama Version

Don't weep for me
If you could see
What I now see
You would not weep . . . you would shout "Victory!"

I know that only sadness now you feel
But, you need to know that Heaven is real
If you could only see the streets of gold, the pearly gate
You would not cry, you might even envy my fate

The skies are always sunny, bathed in God's own light
There is no more rain, no clouds, and no more night
I've left behind sickness, heartache, and pain
No more tears, broken dreams; for now, all is gain

For, here, there is no more sorrow, poverty, or lack
I can tell you now-I don't ever want to go back
Back to the earth, and the trials every day . . .
No, I'll take Jesus, and peace . . . right here I will stay

Don't weep for me now
You don't know what you do!
Don't wish I was there
For if you only knew!

On Thursday, February 14th, at 2:45
It was not that I died, I became alive
I have no more sickness, no more pain
There will be no more clouds, no thunder, no rain

It was no coincidence
That it was Valentine's Day
When the One I most loved took me away
Waiting for you
Here I will stay
The Lord is my Shepherd-Trust Him today

I fought the good fight
The good race I ran
And now I've landed safely
In the bosom of Abraham

For, here in eternity I will forever rest
And walk down these streets with the one called "Blessed"
For I have reached my eternal reward
With the chorus of saints I join in one accord

I don't have time now to shed just one tear
I can only hope that one day, you too, will be here
My body I've left, but why should you grieve?
I've traded it all for this new body I've received

I'm singing right now, and laughing out loud
If you could see me right now, I know you'd be proud
I trusted in Jesus, and Jesus alone
I traded my hospital bed to sit on God's throne

There should be only one reason for you all to cry
And that is to not know where you'll go when you die
For one day you'll die and you'll be right here
But, if you've trusted in Jesus, you'll have nothing to fear

I'll wait, and I'll wait for you to decide
If you don't trust Jesus, then I'll be the one who cried

So, don't weep for me
You know the gospel is true
Follow its course
Lest, from above, I weep for you

So, just remember, if you start to cry
Instead, just look up at that big, blue sky
I'm looking down to tell you again, just like days gone by,
That "God loves you . . . and . . . so do I . . ."

Goodbye Abraham
INTRODUCTION

This was written in memory of my beloved Abraham, the first dog I ever had which I could truly say was "my dog." It seems like we always think of the pain and heartache of losing a pet as being especially painful for children; children who don't "understand what we understand." I don't know how that ever got started. The pain and heartache of losing a member of the family seems even more real, more profound, when you get older. I guess I'm saying that it doesn't get any easier, the older you get. In fact, what makes it so hard is, like Abraham, they were there, by your side, for years and years. You raised them from baby to adult, and each year, you loved and trusted them more. They literally grew from being your child into becoming your trusted friend and constant companion.

I share this for those who have lost their own "Abraham," a dear and trusted friend, who just happened to be a member of the animal kingdom. In my case, this was a dog. But, I have seen that the pain can be just as real and deep, regardless of the species. I love dogs, but I know others who feel the same way about cats, horses, rabbits, and all the other "feathered or furry friends."

Indeed, Abraham was "my dog." When I was outside, he was by my side. When I was working outside, day or night, he would be right there, laying down nearby, but always alert and watching, listening to me. When I moved, he moved. His mate was Sarah, and their offspring was "Baby," whom I wrote about in the "Dear God, I Just Don't Understand" story.

Here's something else that only those of you who have had their own "Abraham" will understand: I still miss him, and, hardly a day goes by, when I don't think of Abraham, or Baby. I still, and it has been many, many years later, miss them. Let's just say that I haven't had another dog since "Baby." I don't know if I ever will . . . as badly as I want one . . .

Goodbye Abraham

Goodbye Abraham
My old and trusted friend
I can see you now running ahead
And stopping just around the bend
Looking back to see if I'll ever catch up
It seems like only yesterday
That you were just a pup

When we brought you home, you were so small
We had to keep you inside the house
You could sleep in your food dish
And, when you cried
It sounded like a mouse

Abraham, my Abraham
I sure miss you
I never realized as you got older
I did too
Down every trail, like a spouse
You'd walk by my side
And now, Abraham, how do I tell my wife?
How do I tell her
That you've died?

He Saw All the Way to Me
INTRODUCTION

This is an example of what Christian writing is, and should do. It tells the story of Jesus. Why and how He came, what happened to Him, and why it matters to me, and to you. Jesus is at the center; in fact, He is what the whole story, the gospel, is about . . . How he came to earth to save me . . . and you. And, as God always seems to be saying, "You've heard the gospel . . . You know it's true . . . Now, what are you going to do about it?"

I had started this story on different pieces of paper, such as worksheets, notepads, and whatever paper I had handy when the next part of the story was revealed to me. I just hadn't gotten the ending yet. One Saturday, I was mowing the grass, out in the middle of the back yard, when the ending came to me. Because of the circumstances, I had no paper, and nothing to write with. And, the ending was coming in several lines! Of course, as is often the case when God tries to give us something, my response was, "God! Why now? Why here?"

I rushed to the wooden shed at the back edge of the yard, slung open the door, hurriedly ran in, my hands shaking, looking for a pencil. I knew I had to have one out there somewhere . . . OK! Got the pencil! But, nothing to write on! Losing the words fast . . . How can I not have paper, anything to write on? "God!!! Help me!!!" Isn't it funny, that when we need God's help the most, it is us who order Him around! I noticed a brown paper grocery bag, folded, on one of the shelves. Bingo! I grabbed the bag, torn off a piece of bag, and wrote what lines I could remember. As the day wore on, I got more and more lines added back to my memory. All afternoon, I followed the same procedure: Remember . . . stop mower . . . run to shed . . . grab scrap of brown paper . . . write a line . . . back to mower. It took the rest of the day, but before I had the lawn mowed, I had all of the lines, including the way "He Saw All the Way to Me" would end.

He Saw All the Way to Me

He came not from Bethlehem
He came from before time began
The infant Jesus just barely opened His eyes
And all eternity came into view
Enriched by a baby's cries
As the baby's eyes opened
And peered past the hay and the straw
It wasn't just the shadows
Dancing off the walls that He saw
There, in the manger, He could see
From Nazareth, to Galilee
To Jerusalem, to Calvary
He could see . . . even then . . .
He could see . . . all the way . . . to me

Inside that feed trough, a manger
God Himself lay curled
His mother, Mary
May have rocked the cradle
But, inside, were the hands
That made, and ruled, the world

"I must be about my Father's business"
He would, even as a youth, say
By age twelve, He was teaching the teachers
And showing the way
That family business that He spoke of
Wasn't carpentry
That business that He spoke of
Was you, and me

He was now thirty years old
A man without food or rest
That's when Satan took notice
And put Him to the test
Satan took Jesus all the way up
To the highest mountain peak
And said, "It's all yours
If you'll just fall at my feet"
When Jesus looked down
All the world He could see
When Jesus looked down
He could see
He could see . . . all the way . . . to me

His vision was clear
It never grew dim
And, He knew that one day
I'd be looking up to Him
It was the first time that Jesus
Ever looked down on anyone
He saw me believing
Believing in God's only son

He would call several dozen
Only one dozen would stay
And, because of those twelve
We are here today

But, they took Him, and they killed Him
For political gain
He was nailed to a cross
After much torture and pain
It would make no difference how much
His followers screamed and cried
God's plan for salvation, through the perfect Lamb
Would not be denied

His beaten, bruised body
Was held aloft for all to see
And, somehow, through the blood and the nails
Jesus still held His grip on eternity
Before He gave up the ghost, He opened His eyes
For one more "look and see"
He looked down past the soldiers
And, from the cross, He could see
He could see . . . all the way . . . to me

It had been three days since Jesus had died
When the angels appeared at the Lamb's tomb side
Jesus, the Savior, was rising from the dead
It was all happening just like He said

With the stone rolled away
Jesus stepped out from the grave
Not just with power over death
But, with power to save
As Jesus took that first step
Having solved death's mystery
He looked out from the tomb
And He could see
He could see . . . all the way . . . to me

His disciples were around Him
As He told them he had to leave
Even though He had just blessed them
Their souls began to grieve
Then, all at once, He began to rise
His feet leaving the ground

Jesus ascended toward Heaven
As they stood, gasping, all around
But, just before He disappeared into a cloud
Jesus took a moment to look down
From His vantage point, high in the sky
So far above hill and tree
He enjoyed the view
As Jesus could see
He could see . . . all the way . . . to me

Jesus came from glory
Starting in swaddling clothes
I may not understand it
But that is the way He chose
Please understand that we could not go to where He was
So, he had to come to where we were

Now, I look back, and consider just why
Jesus would keep looking at me
From the manger to the sky
There is only one reason
That He kept looking at me, and at you
And that is to see what me
And you, would do
There is but one reason
That He keeps looking at you
And that is to see
If you'll make the right choice, too

How Can I Go On?
INTRODUCTION

This is as tough to read, as it was to write.

Here, I combined the concept of being betrayed, with the concept of actually losing your wife to death. For a few moments, I was put in the emotional situation of actually losing your wife . . . I felt it, just like it had actually happened, as I struggled with God, with, yet again, the "Why" questions, coupled with "I just don't understand."

Even now, looking at the words, I cringe. In order to feel the emotion, you have to go there. I have, and I did. I don't want to go there again. However, this was given to me for those who have felt these emotions . . . are even feeling them now. God didn't give me this one for me. It was for those who are in this situation. The whole idea behind this work is to comfort, bring peace, and encourage.

Even though God gave me this to allow me to understand what someone in this situation would be feeling, would be going through, I just can't imagine that degree of pain and mourning.
Oh yeah, I've been betrayed, left to die, put on a raft and left to . . . anyway, we've all been through a lot. And, the bottom line is, and certainly is in my case, God has never left my side. Never. Ever. Not even once. I don't think He ever even thought about leaving me!

God has given me exactly what I needed to "go on" in every situation I have faced. It's ok to have not been in every situation. You can still minister to other people in any situation, because you have been in enough situations of your own, to trust Him in theirs. Period.

Sure, God pulls you out, so that you can go back in to get others. Just as God has "pulled you out," He can pull them out. In fact, He is the only one who can. That's why we have battle scars. As evidence that we have been in battle, made it through, and that we understand what others are facing, even if it is a different battle for them. We don't all have the same scars . . . We just have the same Great Physician . . .

How Can I Go On?

God, I just don't understand
Why you took her away
Is there anything I could have done?
That would have made her stay?

My heart is broken
My bones just ache
Is there anything I could have done?
Could have done for her sake?

I know that you are God
You are in full control
Was it really that important, that necessary
To have her on your roll?

I am so alone
The world is so dark
You took her so soon
She was so alive
And left such a mark

But now, her life is over
And, I feel that mine is, too
I just don't want to live without her
I just don't know what to do

How can I go on?
Take another step?
I know! I'll live without her!
You call that a concept?

And, now I hear your answer
Breaking through my tears
The answer, somehow, I already knew
How I can go on, you say,
Is because
"I will be with you."

RICHARD. VINCENT. ROSE.

I Believe
INTRODUCTION

Many years ago, I was honored to be involved with our Church's monthly food ministry, and each month, I was blessed to preach the Word to three different groups on that particular Saturday morning.

I have always loved the gospel hymns, and I have always thought it would be a wonderful idea to just get up and read the words to these songs, as a type of special reading. I think that we get so used to singing the songs, just like Christmas hymns, we forget just how powerful the words are. So, I was thinking about reading one of the hymns as part of the service, when God spoke to my spirit, and questioned why I didn't just write something of my own to read. So, I did, and "I Believe" became the first real Christian poem which I wrote and shared with an audience.

I read it again, and still, "I believe." I realize that God really does care about us. He cares enough to test what we really do believe. It also reinforces the fact that, many times, when we ask God "Why?" it's not because of a lack of faith . . . it is because *of* our faith . . . and our trust.

I Believe

I believe that Jesus died for me
I believe that He bled . . . and He died
He hung on the cross for all the world to see
And, yes, I believe when God looked on my sin, He cried

I believe that Jesus was placed in a tomb
And a huge rock was put in the door
And then . . . not Jesus, but Satan . . . met his doom
Because God raised Jesus from the dead
And He is still alive today . . . alive forevermore

Yes, I believe that for me, Jesus lived, died, and arose
And I am so glad that it was Jesus that I chose
Because Jesus did not even have to show up!
He did not have to drink from that bitter cup!

I believe it wasn't just for me-He did this for you
So now, dear friend, what will you do?
Will you choose Jesus as your Savior and Lord?
And live forever, with Heaven as your reward?

I Dreamed About Mama Last Night
INTRODUCTION

"I dreamed about Mama last night
Now I know what a saint looks like."

This was written exactly as I remembered it.
It was less than two months after Mama had gone to be with Jesus, when I had the dream described here. It was so clear . . . so vivid . . . I love these "3 Dots" . . . And, I love her.

The dream seemed so real. I woke up, ran to the office, and started to write down what I had seen. The dream started with all of us kids in church . . . and, then, a familiar voice echoed through the pews . . .

All she wanted for us kids was for us to serve the Lord . . . she was such an example . . .

I have said it so many times, and I have heard so many people say it, and I'll write it now:

"She was the closest thing to an angel ever placed on earth."

I Dreamed About Mama Last Night

I dreamed about Mama last night
It's been two months; No, wait! Not quite
It seems like so long ago
Then again, it seems just yesterday
When we saw her go

In my dream, I was in church
I was sitting in the front row
That should have been my first clue
That I was dreaming, you know

Oh, I was raised in church
Together, all six of us kids
Like stair steps in a single row
When the doors were open, we were all there
All of us listening intently
Some of us rocking to and fro

One day, we'll all be back together in Heaven
I'm so glad about that right now
We can say thanks to Mama
She showed us the truth, the way, and how!

But, now, back to my dream
There I was, on the front row
Listening to our Pastor
Our Pastor from that time long ago

He looked as he had looked
When we were all together
There in that row
So real the pictures now seem
From a time so cherished
From a garden from which I would grow

I was listening to Pastor
Even making notes
When, behind me, from the center pew
Came a voice
A voice I loved
I voice I so well knew
I turned and I looked
And saw Mama sitting there
She was reading from Matthew
Her voice filled the church air

I know what you're thinking
Was there something special that she wanted to share?
She was just doing what she always did
Being an example, hoping one day you'd be there

Is there a special message she wanted to impart?
Read your Bible
Stay in church
That is the start

And, I think that was the message
The message was her life
As a mother, a child of her Lord
The way she lived as a wife

Think about it
Don't be sad
She lived the gospel
There's just nothing to add

Stay in church
Read your Bible
Something to impart?
Begin reading about Jesus in Matthew
That'll be a good start

I dreamed about Mama last night
Now I know what a saint looks like

I dreamed about Mama last night
Now I know how someone looks
After they've fought
The good fight

I dreamed about Mama last night
She wasn't just alright
She was more than alright

Let me close by just adding
That Mama would want you to have what she had
So that, one day
You'll get
What she has right now
And, she's right, there's nothing more to say

I Love You Jesus
INTRODUCTION

Don't you hate it when someone hands you a piece of paperwork, looks you in the eye, and says, "Take this. It's self-explanatory." It's never good news.

Once, I was supervisor of the shipping department at a large clothing manufacturing facility. The company changed hands, and during the process, a lot of changes, both in physical appearance, and staff, were happening at rapid speed. During the transition, a lot of extra work was required. Being on salary, you know what that meant. I went through months of 80-plus hour weeks, working through holidays, nights, whatever it took.

As supervisor, I had the clearance to walk throughout the building, including those areas which were off-limits to almost everyone else. One day, I was up in the administration part of the building, during what everyone else in the company was enjoying as a vacation/shutdown week. The fax machine started receiving a fax . . . since no one else was around . . . I waited until the fax had printed, and then grabbed it, with the thought of putting the fax into the recipient's mailbox. Of course, I read it! After all . . . it was a fax, from headquarters, to the plant manager . . . giving the details of how they were going to replace me . . .

Why this story? Why now? First, God brought it to my remembrance to remind me of one of the most important lessons I have learned, and you will see it etched throughout the pages of this volume: "I had no way of knowing it at the time, but what seemed to be the worst thing that had ever happened to me . . . was actually the best thing that had ever happened to me . . ."

It's because Jesus had a plan. A plan for my life. Just like He's got a plan for your life. How can you not love, and serve, a Savior like that?

The "I Love Jesus" song is just that . . . a worship song, which I sang in my head for many years, and was constantly on my lips and mind. I finally wrote it down, and I include it here to encourage you to write down those lyrics . . . those words . . . because . . . you just never know . . .

I Love You Jesus

I love you Jesus
Yes I do
I love you Jesus
Yes it's true

I love you Jesus
You saved my soul
I love you Jesus
You made me whole

I love you Jesus
You died for me
I love you Jesus
You set me free

I love you Jesus
You rose again
I love you Jesus
I'm free from sin

I love you Jesus
By your stripes I'm healed
I love you Jesus
By your blood I'm sealed

I love you Jesus
You turned my world around
I love you Jesus
I'm Heaven bound

I love you Jesus
I'm gonna win this race
I love you Jesus
Then I'll see your face

I love you Jesus
What a great reward
I love you Jesus
Sing in one accord

We love you Jesus
Let the heavens ring
We love you Jesus
Forever we'll sing

We love you Jesus
We love you Jesus
We love you Jesus
We love you Jesus

I Never Did
INTRODUCTION

Over the years, I have written many songs. And, I'll confess, not all of them have been Christian. I have been a writer for most of my life, but I have not served the Lord for my entire life. I've written a lot of songs, poems, short stories, and monologues that were not Christian, but were worldly. I was worldly, so I wrote worldly. I'm not the same person as I was then. That person, thanks to Jesus, no longer exists. I am not the person I once was.

I remember a testimony I heard in church, years ago, and it has stayed with me: "I'm not the person I want to be, but, thank God, I'm not the person I used to be."

I want to share this song/poem with you, for one reason:
What it really says, at its heart, is to not take for granted those you love. Yeah, I know, we all want to do things for those we love. But, you must do them. It's like faith: If you don't show your faith . . . do you really have faith? I think that love, like faith, is an action word. Can you really love someone without showing-by actions-that you love them?

This is the one song/poem in this volume which may be called a "Country Song."
But, it speaks to us all: Show them you love them. How else will they know? Jesus talked about love for His fellow man . . . about faith . . . about power . . . How do we know He had love for His fellow man . . . that He had faith . . . that He had power? Because He demonstrated it!

To those He said He loved, He showed, by His actions, that He really did love them. That includes me and you.

I include this particular work in this volume, to encourage you to tell them . . . show them . . . demonstrate to them, how you feel about them, that you love them.
Don't just be "thinkers," but doers. How else will they know? Think right. Do right.

I Never Did

I thought about sending you flowers.
But, I never did.

I thought about saying I'm sorry.
But, I never did.

I thought about holding you, touching you, loving you.
But, I never did.

I thought about taking you away, so we'd be alone.
But, I never did.

I thought about telling you just how much you mean to me.
But, I never did.

I thought about telling you how I'd be lost without you.
But, I never did.

I thought about telling you how great you looked.
But, I never did.

I thought about telling you how much I love you.
But, I never did.

I thought about telling you just how I feel about you.
But, I never did.

So, when you packed up and left me,
You saw it coming . . .
But, I never did.

In Praise of Pastor's Wife
INTRODUCTION

Now that I had gotten the words for the Pastor and Assistant Pastor, what about the Pastor's wife? After all, besides my Mother (who's best friend was a Pastor's wife), the most Godly women I had ever known were Pastor's wives. Plus, from our online businesses, we were always being asked if we had something for the Pastor's wife.

For 16 years, after writing "Why, Pastor, Why," I had never, not even once, been given anything that even resembled something to write for the Pastor's wife. When I talked with my brother about this, he told me, "If God wants you to write it, He'll give it to you."

How great is God? Remember, there is nothing He can't do, and there's nothing too hard for Him. Then, from "out of the blue," totally out of nowhere, God began to give me the words for something to honor the Pastor's wife. He started to give me the pieces of the puzzle.

There I was, so worried that I couldn't write anything for the Pastor's wife . . . I had no feeling to write anything for over 16 years . . . and, how great is God?
When He had finished, I had five pages of legal pad paper full of notes he gave me!
You don't think God honors the Pastor's wife?
He gives me two separate works to honor them!

One was *"Letter to Pastor's Wife,"* also featured in this volume.
Here is the poem, written in praise of, and to honor, the Pastor's wife.

In Praise of Pastor's Wife

It seems every day, you've had to wear a different hat
And the last thing you'd want is a pat on the back
You've stood so tall, with Jesus and our Pastor both at your side
You have fulfilled every role, as friend, wife, mother, and bride
You and your husband are the models of one accord
And that's just one of many reasons you are so loved and adored
Serving us as unto the Lord
You have given us more than we could ever deserve
You have been the most cherished role model of all
By showing us how best to answer God's call
You have personally been there in good times, great times, and bad
You have been the mother many have wished for, or never had
You made a decision a long time ago
A decision to allow others around you to grow
The kindness and love you have shown
Is the best living example of the Word we have ever known
You have given your life to be a Pastor's wife
The Pastor's wife you chose to be
The image of the Bride of Christ
You'll always be to me
What you mean to this church, and to each and every life
We are so thankful that you chose Jesus, and to be our Pastor's wife
You just want to be a blessing, and, that you have been
If the Pastor, or us, had to choose, we'd both choose you again

I Stopped by Your Place for Christmas
INTRODUCTION

I still remember my tears falling on the paper as I wrote,

> *"I stopped by your place for Christmas,*
> *the place where you always stay . . ."*

Written on the hood of my van, on a torn-apart bank deposit envelope, under a huge maple tree just a few feet away from the grave site of Carol's parents, just hours before a winter storm would cover the ground for months.

I Stopped by Your Place for Christmas

It was one week before Christmas
Exactly, to the day
I stopped by your place
The place where you always stay

The sun was so bright
The sky was so blue
As I stood there and cried
As I stood between you two

The day was so bright
Not a cloud in the skies
As the sunlight glistened
Off the tears in my eyes

I came by your place
To tidy up a bit
Ready to work
All I could do was just sit

I came with some tools
To work on the flowers
Today may be sunny
But tomorrow night, snow showers

It made me think how fast
Life changes from day to day
One Christmas you're here
The next, you're gone away

Gone to a place
We'll all go some day
It made me wonder if people would visit my place
Or would they stay away

As I stood and pondered
Your rose-colored stone
In the midst of a field of monuments
To loved ones now gone

I loved you both and miss you so dear
Another Christmas will come, that I wish you were here
I'll remember that Christmas was your favorite time of year

I thank God for the memories
Of holidays spent
All of us together
I wonder, where has the time went?

I know that one day
We may
Move away
Where ever we go
It is here you must stay

You'll both always be part of our Christmas
We'll remember the love and joy on your faces
And know you'll always be together with us
We'll just spend Christmas in different places

It Took a Judas
INTRODUCTION

Betrayal. Judas. God's plan.

For those of you who have been betrayed by the one closet to you, trust me when I say that I understand exactly, and I mean, exactly, how you feel. But, the most important thing to realize is this: Jesus understands how you feel. He personally showed me why He had stood so close beside me when I was going through this, the most terrible time of agony, suffering, and doubt, which you could possibly go through.

In fact, I couldn't understand why Jesus rushed to my side . . . why He wouldn't leave me . . . at the darkest point of my life . . . It was then that He made me realize why what I was going through meant so much-personally-to Him . . . why it mattered to Him.

I questioned Him, the Lord of Glory, the King of Kings, Jesus . . . I just couldn't understand why He had stayed so close to me, and wouldn't leave me.

"After all," I asked Jesus, "What do you know about this?" My partner in ministry betrayed me, one of my best friends betrayed me, and everyone had turned their back on me when I needed them most.

"Why, Jesus, would you not turn away, like all the others? What do you know about this?"

It was then that He told me: "Who knows more about betrayal, about being betrayed, than me?"

He didn't have to tell me twice. Who *would* know more about betrayal, about being betrayed, than Jesus?

I learned that, what I thought was the worst thing to ever happen to me, was actually the best thing that had ever happened to me. A lesson that only time could teach me.

That, it really did, *"take a Judas to fulfill God's plan."*

It Took a Judas

Oh Lord, please bend your ear
To wailing soul that you hold dear
Oh Lord, please hear my cry
It hurts so bad that I could die

Dear Lord, hear me in my despair
I lift my voice
I know you are there
A promise to never forsake nor leave
My soul, my spirit, consumed to grieve

A traitor from the pit I've found
Compassed by sorrow, their evil knows no bound
All at once I hear your voice
Giving me reason to rejoice

Sackcloth and ashes
Your humble servant waits
Surroundings tremble
As Your voice gravitates

"When the pain is so deep,
And, it hurts so bad,
And, you just don't understand.
Just remember, my child,
It took a Judas to fulfill God's plan."

I Walk (Song of the Walkathon)
INTRODUCTION

This is a simple song in honor of those of you who make the sacrifice to "Walk for a Cause."

Carol and I used to participate in a six mile-plus walkathon every summer, to benefit missionaries. It was held on an oval, paved track, each lap being a quarter-mile, located at the center of the town's recreation complex. The walk always took place in the middle of August, so it was extremely hot, with the steam rising off the pavement. I took special satisfaction in doing the walkathon, as another way to "give the devil a black eye." I remembered times when I could not walk, and dear Carol, whom God had healed of MS . . . finished the walk, "with flying colors," every year. I used to cross the finish line, "stomping a mud hole" in my defeated enemy as I crossed.

I remember Sister Sandy, who arrived at the track, ready to do her "six laps." Somehow, she misunderstood, that the walkathon wasn't six laps . . . it was over six miles. Now, for those of us who have done twenty mile walkathons, six miles may not sound like much. But, Sister Sandy had come to the track after work, dressed in her work clothes, meaning a nice dress. Even in her work clothes, she figured she'd be able to do a mile and a half. She was fair-skinned, wearing a long dress, and the track was an oven. In one of the most incredible acts of grit, stamina, and determination I have ever witnessed, Sister Sandy finished the entire walkathon.

Serving as the "official photographer" for the event, one of my favorite pictures was her racing around the track, red-faced, arms out in the "walker's stance," and the look of determination on her face. And . . . in the middle of the oven . . . it was a look of joy. I'll never forget it.

Somewhere in the world, and in Heaven too, there are people who have heard the Gospel, and responded to it, because of the sacrifices of Sister Sandy, and those like her, that epitomize the spirit of compassion, sacrifice, and endurance.

I Walk (Song of the Walkathon)

I walk because I can
I walk for those who can't even stand
I walk not just because it is fun
I walk because at one time
I could not walk, much less run

Missionaries visit and then go away
But, it is us who stay
Supporting missionaries is just fine
The world needs the Gospel light to shine

The message of Jesus must come first
Overcoming both fatigue and thirst
I remember the walk that Jesus took for me
The walk up Calvary

So, walk a little, walk a lot
Don't forget to take a break
But walk-walk for Him
Not just for the missionary, but
For Christ's sake

I Went to the Altar a Sinner
INTRODUCTION

As a favor to family (sound familiar?), a man goes to church, where he is made uncomfortable by all of the "sanctified eyes" staring at him, a "known sinner." But, God begins to work on him, and, seemingly not under his own control, he makes his way down to the altar. The entire experience is seen though his eyes.

We all have great salvation stories, either of our own experience, or what we've witnessed in services. I'd like to share two of my own:

I was visiting a church during revival, enjoying the powerful message of the guest evangelist. During the invitation, the Pastor's daughter came to the altar, and accepted Jesus as her Savior and Lord. She had been raised in church, and had always done the expected things, including playing piano and teaching Sunday School. She had "gone to the altar" when she was young, too young to understand fully what "accepting Jesus" meant, but it was the expected thing for her to do. But, she understood now . . . that, in spite of everything . . . she still wasn't saved . . .
Suddenly . . . out of the corner of my eye . . . I see another young lady rushing down to the altar . . . running . . . It was the Pastor's other daughter . . . coming down to the altar for exactly these same reasons . . . They both realized that, even though they had been raised in church . . . served in church . . . their father was the Pastor . . . they may have repeated a prayer or something when they were too young to understand it . . . even though they had all of this "going for them," they were just as lost as the man in this story.

The other experience involves my dear brother, and my beloved mother. On a holiday Sunday, just to please his Mother (sound familiar?), my brother agreed to go to church with her. We were raised in church by a Godly Mother . . . then . . . you know the story . . . My brother responded to the altar call, and gave his heart, and life, to Jesus. When he got up from the altar, everything about him was different. Here's why I wanted to share this story: It was something my Mother told him, afterwards.

My brother was a brand new creation, sitting next to my Mother, tears streaming down his face. My brother was scared, really afraid . . . You can imagine, since leaving home, what lifestyle his friends were also living. His concern, as he now looked to his future life, was, "What about my friends?" My Mother looked my brother squarely in the eye, and informed him, "If they really are your friends, they'll still be your friends."

I Went to the Altar a Sinner

I was just an old sinner
When I went to church that day
How I ended up in church
I just can't say
Maybe it was just to please my mother
Maybe because I had seen the difference it made in my brother

Sure, I'd been to church
Off and on through the years
And the Bible?
I'd rather spend Sunday reading the new catalog from Sears

I had grown to hate church, and most of the people I knew who went
I guess because I knew them when they weren't there
When they seemed more Hell-bent
I never trusted them, especially those I had watched through the years
Except those I knew, with whom I could share a few beers

I walked in late, so I thought I would fit in with most
I went right to the back, determined to maintain my post
I thought about making a dash to the stairs
But the ushers in back seemed more like guards in their chairs
I picked up a songbook and flipped through the pages
I could feel people's stares as I kept going back to The Rock of Ages

They sang about what happened on The Old Rugged Cross
And that Jesus would accept me, if I would come, Just as I Am
The people seemed tired and bored, yet interested in the time
I listened more intently than most, for I had forgotten my watch
I wished they'd pay more attention to the preaching
And stop looking at me like I'd committed a crime

I went to the altar a sinner
One of the old songs they sang was that it was Supper Time
And my soul was ready for dinner
I thought I didn't have time for God
My plate was just too full
After all, I had a job, a family, bills to pay,
And my life, well, it had just been too cruel

All through the service
Something kept tugging at my heart
When the Preacher gave the invitation
I just couldn't get my feet to start

Then, with every head bowed and no one looking around
Is there just one more, someone else, who wants to come down?
I waited and waited, hoping for one more chance
Then, all of a sudden my feet began to dance
As the preacher said softly, "I see that hand,"
All of a sudden, I began to stand

All I could see was that empty place at the altar
All I felt was the empty place in my heart
I felt like a horse wearing blinders
My body followed my feet all the way to the front
It was the last thing the preacher said that did it
I didn't want to be one of the "Left Behinders"

I didn't care if anyone else came
I knew that I would never be the same
I found out it was true
About calling on Jesus' name
I knew that Jesus would forgive all my sin
And that, one day, He would come back again
My dreams and my goals suddenly became very dim
As I realized when He came, I'd go back with Him

My cries drowned out the singing
At the altar that day
I didn't want to get up
On my knees I wanted to stay
Because that's where I met Jesus
And He saved my soul
I walked in thinking my life
Had taken too great a toll
I walked in thinking this wasn't for me
Then I realized that Jesus had already paid my fee

I kneeled down knowing who Jesus was
And that He had brought me here
He had paid the price
He was just waiting for my feet to get in gear
I came running to Him
When I realized that, even for me, it wasn't too late
Just like He waited for me at the altar
He would now be waiting for me at Heaven's gate

I went to the altar a professional sinner
But, I came back with Jesus
And, I came back just a beginner

The joy I've found
I wish you knew
I went to the altar a sinner
He's still there
Waiting for you

Jesus Came and Got Me from Cellblock # 9
INTRODUCTION

This is about two types of repentance, and two different types of calls. Certainly, it is the story of a man at the end of his rope, lost in sin, and in need of both salvation and deliverance. He made the right call to the right place! I think of the goodness of God, which leads us to repentance. Then, I am reminded that the gifts and calling of God are without repentance.

I was curious why God chose # 9 for this. I checked into what the number "9" means or stands for. I found that it has at least two meanings: One is to accomplish or fulfill something; the other meaning concerns judgment and final. I also saw a reference to its representation as the best movement of God.

How often I think how, even when we return to a life of sin, God still keeps His hands on us. Even when we are doing stupid things, God still protects and watches over us. When God gives us a calling and purpose for our life, it stays. He doesn't take it away. That's because His covenant promises are based upon Him, not us. His acceptance of us is based strictly on His acceptance of Christ's finished work on the cross, on our behalf. How often I've thought how true it is, that our worst enemy is us. I know that in my life, I have been my worst enemy. There have been times when I have prayed, crying out, "God . . . please save me . . . from me!!!"

So many of us live our lives as prisoners, enclosed in prisons of our own design. Jesus came to set all captives free-even those who are self-imprisoned. I have been blessed to have participated in prison/jail ministries. I have often said, "There are people 'out there' who are just as much in prison as you are. And, just like you, Jesus can save and deliver them, too."

I am so glad that I have answered God's call. Remember, He is the one who calls us first. He is constantly, 24/7, standing by, waiting . . . waiting for us to answer His call. He won't stop calling, even when you try to disconnect. I can promise you that there is one thing which Jesus will always do: Answer the call of a repentant sinner. And, He can be reached from anywhere. His arm is never shortened to where He can't reach, and His ear is never closed to where He can't hear. Jesus is waiting for you to return, and answer, His call.

Jesus Came and Got Me from Cellblock # 9

Midnights used to find me
All drunk and all alone
A picture painted with blurs
And forgotten, sinful scenes
I was a tired old drunken man
A masterpiece in disguise
The landscape is now painted
With the brush of angel's wings

Jesus came and got me
From cellblock # 9
He pardoned all my sins
And even paid my fine
I was given just one chance
To make a final call
So, from my knees I called
To the one that paid it all

He said, I'll forgive you
But, you'll need to trust in me
All I had to give for trade
Was a life torn by sin and shame
I didn't have to pay a ransom
Just trust in Jesus' name

Jesus came and got me
From cellblock # 9
He paid for all my sins
And even paid my fine

I think of Paul and Silas
Alone in a prison cell
All the prisoners heard them
They didn't have to yell
They sang praises to the one
Who had power to set them free
The chains came off, the doors were opened
Just like He did for me

How my life has changed
Since that fateful night
When I thought I had no hope
Like you, I had never done anything right

I went from the king of beers
And those sad songs I would sing
To the one who could calm all of my fears
I went to the King of Kings

My song has now changed
Victory I have won
I set aside my sin
To trust in God's son

I used to trust in the king of beers
My song now joyfully sings
I went from the king of beers
To the King of Kings

Now my children have a father
And my wife now has a man
All because I set aside the frosted mug
And reached out for Jesus' hand

So, if, like me
You are in your own cellblock # 9
There's room in that cell
If you'll just take the time
There's just enough room for Jesus to enter in
He already has the key
He'll be there just to listen
To your words from bended knee
Reach out to Him
Take His nail-scarred hand
The scars were put there
To remove your chains
And to break every band

Jesus came and got me
From cellblock # 9
He'll pardon all your sins
And has already paid your fine
You've been given just one more chance
To make that final call
So, from your knees, place that call
To the one that paid it all

Jesus in the Storm
INTRODUCTION

This is one of my favorites, and I really love the message behind it, which is short, and to the point:

"If Jesus is not in your boat, I don't like your chances of staying afloat."

I have had occasion to council young married couples, and I never miss the opportunity to say this: "You have two choices: Either you can serve God, and go to church together, or you can have problems." I know what you may be thinking, that we all have problems, or troubles. However, I have never had one single person misunderstand what I was really saying: If they don't make God the center of their life . . . get ready for . . . well . . . problems. They always understand.

We always think of Jesus being asleep in the boat, as the storm raged, while His disciples were scared to death. I can honestly say that, in the storms of my life, Jesus was never asleep. He never slept, and never sleeps, even when the winds and the seas are calm. In my case, He's too busy keeping me calm. Jesus never sleeps . . . or slips . . . the controls are always in His hands.

I remember the automobile license plates that, at one time, were really popular, that said, "God is my Co-Pilot." I heard a preacher say, "If that's true, who's the pilot?"

Storm or calm, I want Jesus behind the wheel.
There is an old saying that "Jesus does not promise there won't be storms in your life. But, He does promise that He will be with you in the storm."

Jesus in the Storm

How many times have we been afraid of the storm we are
in . . . When Jesus is right there in the boat with us?

If Jesus is not in your boat
I don't like your chances of staying afloat
So, when the waves are crashing
And water fills the keel
His presence brings calm
His words, "Peace, be still."

God doesn't need us to quiet the sea
He just asks for three little words
"Jesus, Help Me!"
The reason the wind and the waves
Obey His voice
Is because He made them both
They have no choice!

Jesus Meant What He Said
INTRODUCTION

I never really understood how my mother could love all of her children the same way. I mean, she loved each one of us as much as she loved the other. Certainly, she must have a favorite! But, she loved us all the same way . . . what we would call, *"More than anything."* I really never understood the concept until much, much later. I wish I had realized it sooner. There are a lot of things I wish I had realized sooner. Then, when I began to write, I really understood the whole concept.

As a writer, each work that you write, you literally "give birth to." It is a "creation" of yours, which you nurture, "baby," help along the way, always "go back to again and again" to make sure it's still ok, and then, you send it out into the world. When someone asks me which is my favorite poem, song, or story, I can confidently and honestly say, "They all are."

Let's remember that God loves us just as much as He loves Jesus. I'll allow your Pastor to explain that.

Which is your favorite story about Jesus? See what I mean? This poem is a combination of several of my favorite stories about Jesus. I start with Jairus' daughter, move to raising the widow's son in Nain, next to the tomb of Lazarus, and then to the tomb of Jesus. Finally, we move to present day, as Jesus still calls out to those who are dead.

I was able to include one of the favorite lines I use to explain the truth of Jesus, His existence, and His words, especially in regard to the fact that He is, just like He said, coming back: "Everything that Jesus said would happen, did happen . . . even that little bit about rising from the dead . . . So, if He said He's coming back . . . He's coming back!"

We've all heard that "a man's word is his bond." Even in a prison environment, I'm told that "In here, the only thing a man has is his word." Why is it, then, that we have such a hard time believing the words of Jesus? He is The Word. Heaven and earth will pass away, but what will remain? His Word. The Word. And, He meant what He said.

Jesus Meant What He Said

His voice so soft
His voice so sweet
Yet, it has the power
To raise a dead man or woman back to their feet
Jesus meant what He said
He has a voice loud enough
To raise the dead

As the Master was moving
Through the crowd that day
Jairus stopped Him, begging Him
To come without delay
His daughter of twelve
Was sick and in bed
As Jesus was speaking, word came
The damsel was dead
"Be not afraid, only believe"
Was all he did say
Then, he went to the house
Chasing the mourners, and death, away

As he stood before her
Holding life in his hand
He uttered some words
And death could not stand
His voice so soft
His voice so sweet
Yet, it had the power
To raise a dead girl back to her feet
Jesus meant what He said
He has a voice loud enough
To raise the dead

Using just His Word,
And from a great distance away
He had healed the centurion's servant
Now, it's the next day
As they approached a city called Nain
A widow's only son was being carried out
Jesus saw on her face her great sorrow, her pain
What happened next?
Why don't you ask death to explain?
Death heard the same voice
That had stopped the wind and the rain

As Life approached, the words "Weep not"
To the mother were said
He reached out his hand, and had some words
For the man who was dead
"Young man, I say to you arise,"
Was all that was said
But, it was enough
To raise even the dead

His voice so soft
His voice so sweet
Yet, it had the power
To raise a dead man back to his feet
Jesus meant what He said
He has a voice loud enough
To raise the dead

You know what's next
To the tomb of Lazarus we go
It wasn't just a friend who had passed
But four days had passed
And Jesus had arrived at last
Jesus wept when he beheld
Their tears and sorrow
Did they not know
That he also held tomorrow?
He didn't have to be there
In sorrow's dark hour
He came only for the mourners to know
That he held the power
Two were in the tomb
And death would have to go

They rolled away the stone
For more than one reason
They held their breath
He then spoke to Lazarus
In a voice loud enough
To get the attention of death
Three words were all that were needed
But three words that even death heeded
"Lazarus, come forth,"
Said the Resurrection and the Life
Words that conquer above and below
Then, he repeated to them,
Just what he had said to Death:
"Loose him and let him go."

His voice has the power
To raise a dead man back to his feet
Jesus meant what He said
He has a voice loud enough
To raise the dead

Jesus meant what He said
Even though they were dead
They had no choice
They had to obey His voice

Now, it was Jesus
Who was dead in the tomb
But, for death to stay
There just wasn't room
This was going to happen
The disciples were told
Why so shocked when they discovered
The stone was rolled?

It was true
Everything Jesus had said
Including that part
About rising from the dead
Once again, death was defeated
No further explanation should be needed
Only His Words should be heeded

There I was
Dead in my sin
When I heard that soft, sweet voice
Calling out to me again
I was lost in sin and had become a doubter
Jesus took me in
And His voice was louder

Jesus meant what He said
Even though I was dead
I had no choice
I had to obey His voice

Come unto me, and I will give you rest
All this time, His power has passed every test
I took up His yoke; I could bear no more
Jesus was standing at my eternity's door
He forgave all my sin
Just like He said
And brought this man back to life
A man that was dead

Jesus meant what He said
With a voice loud enough to raise the dead
I believe He's coming back like He said
When we all hear the trumpet sound
The saints will rise first from the ground
Yes, all my sainted loved ones will be there
And, we'll all meet Jesus in the air

Jesus meant what He said
He has a voice loud enough
To raise the dead
Shouldn't you accept Him?
Hear what He has to say?
I mean, when He speaks
Even death has to obey
His Word has the power to raise the dead
Don't you think you should listen to what He said?
He can raise a dead man, a dead woman,
A dead daughter, a dead son
Shouldn't you obey Him?
After all that He has done?

Just Say the Word
INTRODUCTION

I wrote this one on the back of an electric utility work sheet, and finished it on the back of a work memo. This is a call to witness, to "just say the word" to others . . . others who may just be waiting for us to share the gospel with them.

It is another combination of some of my favorite stories about Jesus, and emphasizes that Jesus was, living and breathing, the very Word of God. It begins "In the beginning," then moves to the streets of Capernaum. This is the story involving the centurion, and would be just one day before Jesus would walk the streets of Nain. We included the great story of blind Bartamaeus, and then we visit the tomb of Jesus. Once again, we look ahead to Jesus' return, but, in the mean time, the call is clearly there to speak the Word to those we meet. The call for the Living Word, which is inside us, to "come forth" to reach the lost around us.

Only God knows how many people we already know, and those whom we will meet, who are just waiting to hear what we have to say . . . the Word. To speak it . . . we must live it . . . just like Jesus did.

Just Say the Word

In the beginning
There was darkness and void
Nothing existed
But the Word of the Lord
Nothing there
Not even air
Nothing could be heard
Then came the sound of God's Word

God's Word came walking
Through Capernaum one day
He met a centurion
Along the way
His servant was sick
Dying, tormented by pain
Jesus must come quickly
For, tomorrow, His steps would take Him
To the town of Nain

As the soldier pleaded
His faith was revealed
Jesus did not have to travel
He could just say the Word
And his servant would be healed
Feeling not worthy to have the Master under his roof
When the centurion went home
He had his proof
He had found the man of which he had heard
A man who could heal
By just saying the Word

Bartamaeus could not see
But he could hear
And he could tell
When Jesus came near
He cried out to Jesus
"Have mercy on me
Thou Son of David
That I may see.
Thou, Jesus,
Don't leave me behind
Just say the Word
And I'll be no more blind
If you will
Just speak the Word to me
Just say the Word
Then, I'll be able to see."

Three days in the grave
Nothing was heard
Jesus was waiting
For God to just say the Word
Night then turned into day
The stone was rolled away
At the sound of His Word,
Darkness had to find a new place to stay

As the Word came forth
The Word stepped forth

Jesus is waiting for God
To just say the Word
A Word that's never been spoken
A Word that's never been heard
Then, He will split the eastern sky
And we'll go with Him to a land
Where we will never die

Just say the Word
I'll fly like a bird
Across the shore to heavens above
To spend forever with the one I love

When trials and tribulations come my way
There is hope and victory through what I can say
And when trouble and heartache come against me
I can just say the Word
And even Satan has to flee

I can speak His Word
Because I have the Word
Living inside
Not only a comfort
But a guide
A living Helper
Showing me the way
Could it be that my friends are waiting, listening
For what I could say?
Could they be waiting for me?
To just say the Word?
A Word that would give them hope and a victory
"Just say the Word," they may think, and not say
I may have just what they need
Just for them, just for today
Lord, please help me to speak what I've heard
Lord, for their sake, please help me
To just say the Word

Just Wait (The Streets of Nain)
INTRODUCTION

I am so glad that God gave this one to me. God allowed me to go back to the streets of a village called Nain, where Jesus would raise the widow's son from the dead. I saw it, I felt it, and I wrote it. This is one of the works which took over ten years to complete.

Years ago, when I was reading electric meters for various utilities, God gave me the beginning. I wrote the first stanza on the back of a sheet where we would write down the meter readings, as we helped someone finish their route. This was a common practice, to help someone finish on time. As another meter reader would "read the route," I would start at the end of the route, and work back, writing down the readings.

Years later, God gave me the rest of the work. I was really there, for I had to be, in order to know their feelings and thoughts. However, in order to "take me there," God had to put me in different circumstances and trials, in order to get the whole idea behind the story.

It is a "tour de force" of something God is trying to tell us: To not give up . . . no matter the circumstances . . . don't give up . . . He's not yet through . . . Just wait . . . when you least expect it . . . He's not done yet . . .

I dedicate this to so many of you who are facing trials, and many who have lost hope . . . Your hope is exactly the same hope which the widow of Nain had . . . Your hope is Jesus, and what He can do . . . He hasn't lost any power . . . and, He loves you . . .

It also gives the clear message that, when you least expect it, He'll come back. I remember wondering if, on the streets of Nain, when Jesus stepped forth, did He appear from out of the East?

Then, God showed me something really amazing: How would the mother, "the widow of Nain," introduce her son, years later? And, what words would she have for you, today? Here they are.

Just Wait (The Streets of Nain)

Just wait
I'm not yet through
Just wait
Have faith
And one day
I'll be coming back for you
So be watching
Be waiting
Be looking
To the East
Just wait
I'll be back
When you expect it
The least

Down the road came the mourners
All dressed in black
The broken-down widow
Knew her son would not be back
The mourners all weeping
Their cries so sad and so loud
When all at once a man
Stepped out from the crowd
He spoke not a word
Until he reached the bier
All eyes were upon Him
Every ear
Strained to hear

Just wait
I'm not yet through
In the middle of nowhere
I came here for you
Just wait
Have faith
I'll be there
After all hope has ceased
Just wait
I'll be there
When you expect it
The least

The hand of God reached out
Just like it's reaching out today
The Creator is still working
With His favorite form of clay
The hand of God is still reaching
Bringing life to the dead
One day all eyes will again be on Him
As they remember what He said

Just wait
I'm not yet through
When it seems all hope has ceased
I'm here reaching for you
Just wait
Have faith
I'll be there
When you expect it
The least
I wonder, if that day,
He stepped forward from the East?

Now, back to the village
Nain, it was called
A man had stepped forth
As the widow's son was being palled
Pulled through the town
But now stopped in the middle of the road
The horses didn't know it
But soon, Jesus, would lighten their load
They didn't know why
But all the people stood still
In just a few moments
A once distant God
Would become very near, very real
A dead son's mother
A dead man's wife
Would soon come face to face
With the Giver of Life

The hand of God reached out
In mercy
Touching the bier
The Lawgiver overruled the Law
He touched the unclean
And He did it without fear
All ears were now open
Wide open their eyes
They saw
They heard
"Young man, I say unto thee, arise."

What happened next
They talk about still
The report would resound
Through every valley
Over every hill
Down every road
Over every peak
As he that was dead
Sat up
And began to speak
He had no father,
No sister, no brother
But, Jesus had compassion
On his dear, sweet mother
Yes, He had done this
For his mother's sake
But, before He could leave
A delivery He must make

Delivering the son into his mother's arms
The Giver of Life had done this
When he was born, years before
But, this second time
In front of the town,
It meant so much more
This man had to be the Son of God
He could be no other
As He delivered the one who was dead
Back to his Mother

I've often wondered how, years later
The mother would introduce her beloved son
We don't know what the mother said
But it had to be something like
"This is my son, who once was dead
But is now alive
Because of seven words
That someone once said"
I wonder if, when approached by troubled friend
Someone, perhaps at their rope's end
How this aged mother would explain
What happened that day on the streets of Nain

"Just wait
He's not yet through
He's here reaching for you
Just wait
Have faith
When it seems all hope has ceased
He'll be there
When you expect it
The least
Jesus is Lord
Over famine and feast
So, be expecting
What you expect
In the least"

Letter to Assistant Pastor
INTRODUCTION

It had been several years since I had held the pen for "Why, Pastor, Why."

God had given me the idea for something just as significant for the Assistant Pastor, and I had kept the first words tucked away in a drawer. In the back of my mind, for years and years, I knew that, after writing "Why, Pastor, Why," the natural next step would be to write something for the Assistant Pastor. I just didn't get all of the words until sixteen years later. Yes, sixteen years. "Why, Pastor, Why" had kept us so busy, that I didn't have the time, or inclination, to get back to something for the Assistant Pastor.

God gave me the words to "Letter to Assistant Pastor" in a variety of different locations, over those sixteen years, so I wrote the words on just as varied types of paper. I had some notes written on note cards, "sticky notes," memo pads, and note pads. Yes, it took sixteen years to sit down and put them all together. Then, it was time.

What God gave me was not a poem, as with "Why, Pastor, Why." I didn't know "why" until the very end. The work to honor Assistant Pastors was not even a poem. It was a letter. I wrote the letter, written from the Pastor to the Assistant Pastor, and then . . . I got the ending. The ending that surprised even me! All these years, I just didn't know. You'll have to read the "Letter" to find out what I am talking about.

Haven't we all known such wonderful Assistant Pastors? The words fit those I have been so blessed to have known. And, I hope those you have known.

In this volume, we have included the original "Letter to Assistant Pastor," in its entirety, just as it was given to me, and then, we include the condensed version, in order to make it available as a plaque or print presentation.

Here's a new quote God gave me, just for the Assistant Pastor:

"Jesus needs an Assistant Pastor. And, so does the Pastor."

Letter to Assistant Pastor
Full Version

My Dear, Faithful, and Beloved Assistant Pastor:

For a long time now, you have knowingly, and willingly, stayed in the shadows, out of the spotlight. You have faithfully served me, while staying under my shadow. You have never complained about me getting "top billing." In fact, you seemed to always take extra joy when I was exalted, when I was praised. Even for work that you had done. You always made sure that my name, not yours, was mentioned; that I got the credit.

You have worked all hours of the day and night to make sure that my goals were met. You would make sure that all of the congratulations, the reward, went to me. If you did not succeed, you would never mention my name in a negative way. You would take the blame. The only time my name was mentioned was to praise me for being with you every step of the way, for giving you encouragement to keep the faith. Your faith in me never faltered.

Even in despair, you would talk openly about how I was now helping you back up from failure, and how I was the one who would give you the help and encouragement to keep trying. You've wept, you've cried, wondering why I haven't done more. Then, you realized that, many times, my plan was not to change the church-it was to change you.

You have made so many sacrifices of yourself, and your family, in order to serve me, and my family. I know that there were times you thought, "Let someone else clean it up, pick it up, get here 45 minutes before service, take the offering, give up days off, and give up family vacations for camp or conference." But, you never said it.

Whatever trial you were going through, you never, ever, lost your faith in me. You were never afraid to come to me for help, or advice. And, even if, in your heart, you did not always agree with my suggestions, you always followed them. Sometimes, even blindly, always trusting that

I had what was best for you in mind. You may have questioned, or not fully understood my judgment, but you never argued with my decisions.

Many times, I have asked you to speak for me, in my place. Many of those times, when you faithfully "stood in" for me, it was very difficult for you. I know that so many of those times when you stood behind the pulpit in my place, you were going through trials of your own. It took great courage and faith to deliver a message that you would find out, later, was really meant for you.

I know my shadow is large. But, even if you had to keep moving, your only desire was to make sure you stayed underneath it. I've known that, all along, some people have thought that you've stayed covered, even suffocated. Please know that you, and your dreams, haven't been smothered. They've been covered. With prayer and protection.

When life was at its toughest, you've felt like that shadow had overtaken you. It had. It was my shadow. That's why, when things were at their worst, you felt my presence so strongly. You felt that I was so near. It's because I was.
I haven't held you back.
I've held you up.

You're right. You have been living in someone's shadow, the whole time. My shadow.
Remember that you are not his assistant. You are my assistant.
You are not working for him.
You are working for me.

Thank you for your praise, your thanksgiving, your dedication, your faithfulness, your patience, and your life.

Signed, with eternal love,

Jesus

Letter to Assistant Pastor
Plaque/Print Presentation Version

My Dear, Faithful, and Beloved Assistant Pastor:

You have faithfully served me, while staying under my shadow,
making sure that I got all the praise, even for work you had done.
You have worked all hours to make sure my goals were met.
Your faith in me never faltered. Often, you've cried, wondering
why I haven't done more. Then, you realized that, many times,
my plan was not to change the church-it was to change you.
You have made many personal sacrifices, to serve me, and my family.
You never lost faith in me. You were never afraid to come to
me for help or advice. Even if you did not always agree, you
always followed, trusting that my plan was best for you.
Many times, you have spoken in my place. Often, this was
difficult, because you were going through trials of your
own. It took great courage and faith to deliver a message
that you would find out, later, was really meant for you.
I know my shadow is large. But, you have
been careful to stay underneath it.
You, and your dreams, haven't been smothered.
They've been covered. By me.
When life was toughest, you felt like a shadow had overtaken you.
It had. It was my shadow.
I haven't held you back. I've held you up.
Yes, you have been living in someone's shadow. My shadow.
Remember that you are not his assistant. You are my assistant.
You are not working for him. You are working for me.
Thank you for your dedication, faithfulness, patience, and your life.

Signed, with eternal love,
Jesus

Letter to Pastor's Wife
INTRODUCTION

"Hey! I'm a guy! How am I ever going to write this?"
Carol reminds me, once again, "Who writes it?"
I reply, "God does. I just hold the pen."

So, I, a man, begin to answer the call of writing something
just for the Pastor's wife. Please see the introduction to "In
Praise of Pastor's Wife" to see how this came to be.

As I have mentioned, it took sixteen years to write "Letter
to Assistant Pastor." If God wanted me to write something
in honor of Pastor's wife, He'd give it to me.
He gave me "In Praise of Pastor's Wife," and
then, He gave me a second work!

However, this one was different. In the same way He gave me
"Letter to Assistant Pastor," He gave me a letter, written from a
dear friend, to the Pastor's wife. And, just like the letter written to
the Assistant Pastor, it ends with a twist! I didn't know until the
very end, how this letter would end . . . It was so different from
the Assistant Pastor Letter . . . And, it surprised even me! You'll
understand why, when you read the "Letter to Pastor's Wife."

"No greater example of Jesus I've seen
Than the example my Pastor's wife has been."
R.V.R.

Letter to Pastor's Wife

To my beloved Sister _____:

I'd like to share how wonderful you have been to me and my family, and how grateful I am to have you in my life. My feelings of gratitude are so deep that I thought it best to write my feelings down. You have been my closest, dearest, and most trusted friend. You have shown me how to have a life filled with faith, love, and hope. You have given your life to serve and teach me, by both your example, and your words. You have stood beside our Pastor, our church family, and me. You have interceded for me, my family, and my friends. Regardless of the time, day or night, you have been there for me. Whenever I needed your help, your guidance, or just your ear, when I cried out to you, you always answered. Often, you would listen to me, and talk to me, when no one else would. Even before I knew you personally, you accepted me, and seemed so joyful when I finally accepted you. From the very start, when I needed you, you were never afraid to come to where I was, to meet with me. I have learned, through your love and faithfulness, to trust you completely. You have been such an influence on me, my children, and my entire family. Your have given us hope, encouragement, and most of all, love. You have helped me overcome my past, and shown me what a wonderful future God has for me, and given me a reason to go on. I promise to continue to lean on you for strength, wisdom, and guidance. I love you, and I thank you for all you've done for me.

In closing, I must confess that, at first, I was writing this letter to Jesus. Then, I realized that all of the words that I had written to Him, I could write exactly the same words about you. After all, you have been the one person who is the most like Jesus, in both your words and your actions. I'm sure Jesus wouldn't mind if I gave this letter to you instead, because, after all, He was the one who sent you to our Pastor, to our church, and to me.

From Proverbs 31, it is us, who rise up, and because of you, we can be called "blessed."

Lord, I Want to Thank You for a Mama That Prayed
INTRODUCTION

It took me several years to finish this, though the title rang like a chorus through my mind for all of those years. This is a completely true story in song. Mama never wished fame for us; only that we would serve God with our lives.

I added many of the things she would say, including things like "Honor Him and He will honor you," which, all through my grown-up years, she would encourage me with. This saying made such a strong, lasting impact on me that our first online business, Pastor Appreciation Gifts, which sprang from "Why, Pastor, Why," used "To Honor Those Who Honor Him" as part of our company logo.

Of all that I've written to honor my mother (and, by so doing, honoring all Godly mothers), this is one of my favorites, because it is so true, and the words really tell the story. Mama had four boys, so she spent a lot of time on her knees. I also included a favorite reference to Psalms, which was her favorite book. The phrase "The Lord is my Shepherd, trust Him today" is such a part of her, that I also included it in the special "Mama Version" of "Don't Weep for Me."

When I present this to a church audience, I always add, "How many of us are here today because of a Mama that prayed? And, would not stop praying for us?"

> "The first gift, and the best gift that God gives a child
> is a loving, Godly mother. The first view of Jesus that
> a child receives is through her loving care."

> "The first time I ever saw, felt, or heard Jesus,
> was in your eyes, in your arms,
> and in your voice."
> R.V.R.

Lord, I Want to Thank You for a Mama That Prayed

Lord, I want to thank you
For a Mama that prayed
And from your path
She never strayed
Lord, I want to thank you
For a Mama that prayed
No matter how tough the times got
From your path
She never strayed

Lord, times were tough
And the days were long
But Mama wore a smile
As she taught us this song

"Honor God and He will honor you
Trust in God because His Word is true
You'll have a home in Glory
And with Him you'll stay
The Lord is my Shepherd
Trust Him today"

She prayed not for riches,
Nor diamonds, or gold
All the time
Laying up treasures untold

For all of her children
She prayed not for wealth or for fame
But that each one of us
Would just honor His name

"Honor God and He will honor you
Trust in God because His Word is true
You'll have a home in Glory
And with Him you'll stay
The Lord is my Shepherd
Trust Him today"
She never turned her back on God
The Bible, or on me
I first learned about Jesus
While I was at her knee

And all of the times from his Word I would stray
I didn't know why God would keep me this way
God honored His Word, and kept me alive each new day
All because on her knees she would stay
My life kept on because of a Mama that prayed

She was small in stature
Sometimes weak, sometimes frail
But, she prayed to a God
She knew would not fail
I look back now, and see her bended knee
Praying for me, taller than any tree

"Honor God and He will honor you
Trust in God because His Word is true
You'll have a home in Glory
And with Him you'll stay
The Lord is my Shepherd
Trust Him today"

There are so many millions
Who are in Heaven today
Who would not be there
If not for Jesus
And a mother that prayed

So, let's all stand
Those of you, here today,
Who would not be here,
If not for a mother that prayed

"Honor God and He will honor you
Trust in God because His Word is true
You'll have a home in Glory
And with Him you'll stay
The Lord is my Shepherd
Trust Him today"

And, when I get to Heaven
His face I shall see
I'll look into His eyes
And thank Him for the one who prayed for me

Lord, I want to thank you
For a Mama that prayed
And from your path
She never strayed
Lord, I want to thank you
For a Mama that prayed
No matter how tough the times got
From your path
She never strayed

"Honor God and He will honor you
Trust in God because His Word is true
You'll have a home in Glory
And with Him you'll stay
The Lord is my Shepherd
Trust Him today"

Love Notes
INTRODUCTION

I wanted to add to the volume this small collection of short notes which I've saved over the years. These are just what the title implies, "love notes:" very short poems, beginnings of poems or songs, or just statements which I wrote down, and for whatever reason, did not expand upon the thought or idea into a longer work. These are ones which I really did just "make up" and write down.

Some of the short rhymes or statements stand alone as written, without anything further needed to be added. You may consider some of these as "starters" for something you'd like to write, or just use them in your own circumstances, "as is."

It seems fitting that with a collection of "Praise Songs and Love Messages," we'd want to include at least a small group of "love notes." It is still ok to really love your wife, and even slip her a little note to that effect . . . I don't care how old you are, finding a note that just says "I love you" on the dresser, or in your lunch, etc. . . . . it just doesn't get old. In fact, things like that have a way of making some things new again . . .

Hope you enjoy them.

Love Notes

As for me
I care not what the future holds
As long as I'm holding you

If ever, anything
Was meant to be
It was you
Loving me

Here's your answer to when she says, "You still here?"
"As you can see, I haven't moved much. That's
because I was hoping you'd be back."

There's something about the way you look every night.
At me.

You are the best thing I ever did for me.

You would make burlap sparkle.

You're my spring song
The one I've waited for
For so long

When it comes to loving you
I'm a true enthusiast

In your arms
Is where I'll be
Me loving you
You loving me

I finally found something
More beautiful than the mountains
Something that I'd rather see
For, you are more beautiful
Than the mountains to me

When I look in your eyes
I can see forever
I can see me
It's forever
That I can see
In your eyes
Me

I want you to know
That God's promises are true
I want you to know
That I really do love only you

You took away my past
You gave me a future that will last
And I'm going to love you in every way
I'm going to love you
Like there was no yesterday

I want to experience everything with you
Everything I've ever done that I've enjoyed
I want to do it again
With you

I don't have to go outside
To see stars
I can stay inside
In your arms
And just look
Into your eyes

I thought I knew what beauty was
I thought I knew what faithful was
I really thought I knew what love was
Until I met you

You are a diamond
In my eyes
And I live for the sparkle
In your eyes

Where will I be
In the future?
I know where I'll be
In your arms

There's only one thing
I want to hear from you
And that is
What you need
Consider it done

Everything we've done
Was better
Because I did it
With you
Everywhere we've been
Was better
Because I was there
With you

R.V.R.

Master of the Sea, Master of Me
INTRODUCTION

Here, I used the age-old analogy of life being a stormy sea, to tell the story of a sinner's repentance, salvation, and deliverance. This is a common theme of my writing, and, well should be.

Still today, God's greatest miracle is not the oceans, or the planets, or the mountains. It's how He can take the lowliest of sinners, who have no hope or future, and change them into something beautiful, and their lives into something even more beautiful. And, He can do it fast!

When I pray, I find great joy in telling God how great He is. There is nothing He can't do, and nothing is too hard for Him. As Creator, He made the stars, the mountains, the planets, etc. I am constantly reminding God, when I look at the mountains which surround us up here in the Great North Woods, "If you can make that mountain, then you can do this!" I just take such joy in praising God for how great He is. For some reason, and, I can't really explain why, the fact that He is the one who tells the oceans "That's far enough!" brings me to joyous laughter when I pray. Maybe because it's so obvious, but His control over "the wind and the waves" just brings me such joy. Perhaps, it's because He has mastered so many storms in my life, that the ocean's obedience to His word is such a powerful witness. A witness which displays His power around the clock, around the world . . . which, by the way . . . He created, too.

The first part of the title represents who Jesus is . . . the second part represents who I want Him to be.

Master of the Sea, Master of Me

On life's stormy ocean, I was tossed about
The storm against me so angry
Life's raging tide had compassed me
It was all I could do just to stay afloat
I knew it was my last watch
As I was thrown completely out of the boat

I cried out to God
From the middle of the sea
"I can't make it any longer
Lord, please save me!"

The storm had won
I had no strength left
I would die, right here in the sea
When, from out of the raging storm
I heard a voice saying, "Peace, be still"
I knew He was speaking to me

I thought I was breathing my last
I came up just long enough to see
Jesus, walking, walking toward me
He was walking across the raging sea!
He reached out His hand
And He saved me

He reached out His hand
The storm still raged, but He was so near
I was sinking fast
When I heard, "Have no fear
For, I am here"

Even today, when worries and troubles
Make the light seem so dim
I know in my heart
I can still reach out to Him

When the storms of life toss you about
When all you can see are the wind and the waves
Just remember His words
And, that Jesus still saves

He will guide you safely
Back to the shore
This storm, too, will pass
You'll see, He'll be there
Just like before

Even the wind and the waves
Recognize His voice
And, so do I
Safe in His arms, I rejoice

Jesus is still Master of the raging sea
Jesus, I want you to be
The Master
The Master of me

Millions
INTRODUCTION

This is a love poem, written by someone who was amazed that someone so beautiful could love them. I wrote this, many years ago, for Carol. I was a Spirit-filled Christian, and I was in love with the woman who would become my wife.

This is one of those works which I really had to think about, before including it here. This tells you how I had been influenced so wrongly by the world's ways. I love Jesus. With all of my heart, mind, soul, and strength. I love Carol. With all of my heart. Why should I be "timid" about sharing that? I guess it's because there is a thought that if I love another human being "with all of my heart," that would take away from my love for Jesus. Where did I get that? I have been in churches where any display of emotion was considered wrong. Where you couldn't applaud in appreciation for someone who had just sang their heart out for God . . . and, for me. I have been in churches where the men sat in one place, and the women sat in another. Sorry, I always thought that was wrong. That "being totally in love with my wife" was some sort of secret sin . . . which you did not want to exhibit-or even talk about in front of other Christians.

I can even remember a time when, during a wedding ceremony, the preacher would always remind the attendees that marriage was the first institution God created . . . even before the church.

When I am in church, I sit with Carol. Period. Honestly, I don't even want to speak or perform unless she is in the audience. Never. Ever. Carol is my biggest fan. And, always has been. As I've written, when I come up, Jesus is on one side, and Carol on the other.

Here is something I have said often, and repeat it here, in writing: This is for husbands: If your wife is not your biggest fan . . . you've got problems.

For wives: If your husband is not your biggest fan . . . you've got problems.

I jokingly refer to this work as being written so long ago . . . that, if I wrote it today, I would have to change the title to "Billions."

Still . . . the subject, and its meaning, would be the same.

Millions

I've had a million hopes and dreams
I've had a million deals and schemes
You are more than a million dreams come true
You are the one
It's just me and you
You are so much more than a dream
You are so beautiful, my life to redeem

The look in your eyes
Oh, so blue!
What I see is my life
Just me and you

I'm not worried about millions
Only one
I'm not worried about millions
Or, what you've done
Nothing but future
There is no past
Only our love
And, that will last

What's happened before
Does not happen now
Making my love for you soar
Soar to new levels, soar to new heights
Because, this time, I finally got it right

The look in your eyes
The look on your face
Makes all past disappear
Makes all memories erase

Gone are the millions
There is only one
There is only one winner
When our race is won

You are the best thing
That's ever happened to me
No more are the millions
Only two were meant to be

My hopes and dreams
Have finally come true
All my hopes and dreams
Are realized with you

Yes, my dreams have now come true
There may be millions
But, I love only you

Not Since Judas
INTRODUCTION

Not since Judas, I thought, has anyone been betrayed this completely
Not since Judas, I thought, has anyone hurt this deeply.
R.V.R.

I didn't add the lines written above to "Not Since Judas," because, frankly, I didn't write them until now. These are two lines which I lived, I experienced, and I overcame. I hate to say it, but it does have a nice rhyme to it. It's exactly how I felt, and what I thought. If you've been there, you understand completely.

The key is *"I thought."* When a personal tragedy happens to you, you really think . . . you really believe . . . that no one has ever had this happen to them, or hurts the way you do. You think you are the only one who has ever gone through something like this. I know, because that's the way I felt when I went through my own personal tragedy of betrayal, perpetrated by the person closest to me.

However, the world, and history, is full of people, both men and women, who have suffered exactly the same circumstances, and experienced exactly the same feelings. As you know, I realized . . . later . . . that, what I thought was the worst thing that had ever happened to me . . . turned out to be the best thing that ever happened to me.

Why write about it? Why talk about it? Because of this:
When Jesus was betrayed by Judas, this led to the worst thing that ever happened to Jesus . . . but, that wasn't the end of the story, was it? In many ways . . . it was only the beginning. The beginning of what He was really sent to earth to do, to accomplish. It could not have happened without this "beginning." Without this terrible, horrible beginning, the rest . . . what you were sent here to do . . . would not have happened . . .
As in "It Took a Judas," it really did *take a Judas to fulfill God's plan.*

I write about it to let you know that I understand what you are going through. I understand about the betrayal, of friends deserting you, of being left alone to die, the loneliness, the pain, and the doubt and confusion. And . . . if you really are called . . . why did this happen? I remember that one! Jesus heard the same sorts of cries and mockery: "Hey . . . if you really are . . . then, why is this happening to you . . ." Jesus, and me, and now you, understand all this. Jesus understands this more that anyone who has ever lived. That's why He was so close to me during my time, and that's why he will be so close to you during your time.

"Hey . . . if you are really called, if you really are who and what you say you are . . . then, why is this happening to you?"
Because . . . it had to.

Now, I can help you. Help you out. I don't mean "help you out" in a nice polite way, but, literally, help you "out" of it. As in "lead you out;" as in "I've been there, I made it through, and now I'm coming back for you" help you out.

I think I just wrote another two lines:

> *I've been there, I made it through*
> *And now I'm coming back for you.*

> *"I don't write about tragedy or loss . . . I write about comfort, victory,*
> *and great gain."*
> *R.V.R.*

Not Since Judas

Not since Judas
Has the betrayal been so complete
Satan himself drew from the well of defeat
To bring up not one, but two, buckets of deceit

Not since Judas
Two pawns with a goal so low to achieve
Someone so much in love would be so easy to deceive
The rug that was pulled out from under
Carried the devil's own weave

Not since Judas
Had the river of deception run so deep
There were so many broken promises to keep
It was said from the heavens, that again, Jesus did weep

Not since Judas
Did such an enemy utilize a kiss
The hoax so perfect, no one suspected anything amiss
What appeared as the peak of loyalty
Became the bottomless pit of faithlessness

Not since Judas
Is the outcome so clear
The beginning of wisdom
Should be to fear

As both betrayer, and betrayed
Ended up hanging on a tree
Both examples
For all the world to see
One marked the beginning of sorrows
One made possible all my tomorrows

Not since Judas
Has there been such a bitter cup
The plan was for all of history to disrupt
But, take a look where Judas
And, the one he betrayed
Ended up

You ask me why, after so long
Has the pain still stayed?
Remember, after 2,000 years
Jesus still bears the scars of one betrayed

Not since Judas
How could it have happened to me?
Jesus will carry those scars
For all of eternity

Scars, someday, I'll see

Our Love Was Meant to Be
INTRODUCTION

I trust that you will find this metaphoric in spots, thinking about how Jesus loves us, and takes us as His own . . . regardless of what we've done.

Isn't that the meaning of unconditional love? It's like an unconditional covenant. Its promises are not based upon the one being promised, but upon the one who promises. That's just how Jesus loves us. It doesn't matter who we were . . . it matters who He is!

We are to love our wives just as Jesus loves the church. This is one truth that I really know about, and understand. This is why I can see both Jesus, and my wife, within the words.
I have always felt, as someone who has experienced such pain, grief, and tragedy . . . which led to such joy . . . that it is no coincidence that the book of Psalms follows Job. Then, Proverbs follows Psalms. Job leads to Psalms, which leads to wisdom . . . Proverbs. No coincidence.

When I think of the book of Job, I think of a story told by a housekeeper, employed at the White House, during Abraham Lincoln's presidency. She noticed that, time after time, day after day, President Lincoln sat and read a particular book. It was always the same book, and it looked like it was always the same section of the book. One day, she couldn't stand the curiosity any longer. She waited until the president had finished reading from the book, and had left the room. She anxiously walked over to see what book had captured the president's repeated attention. It was the Bible. And, it was opened to the book of Job.

I find it amazing, and it really is a coincidence of alphabetization, that in this volume, the poem about Judas, detailing what I personally refer to as "The Saddest Story Ever Told," is followed by "Our Love Was Meant to Be."

Our Love Was Meant to Be

No matter what's happened
No matter what you've done
I want you to know
I love only one

I am not them
They are not me
That life is gone, lost forever
I want you to see
You love only one
And that is me

Mistakes are made
There seems no way out
Then, you see a different route
I want you to know
I love you now, I loved you then
I love you now
A love without sin

No questions
No lies
No one other
No need for alibis

For you are the one I want
The one I live for
The one I love
The one I adore

I don't care what's happened
I don't care what has been
I know this is true love
A love I will defend

I don't care what has happened
I don't want to know
Yet, to tell me everything
Is to bare your soul

To share with me everything
Lets our souls intertwine
Then I will know
That you are really mine

So, bare your soul
Tell only me
Then we will both know
Our love was meant to be

Panic, Prayer, Preparation
INTRODUCTION

This is where the "Three C's" meet the "Three P's."

I have, just like you, worked with many people whose first response to any given situation is to panic. It has always seemed like I was the one expected to keep cool, calm, and collective (which I remember as the "Three C's").

A favorite saying I have, when something "breaks out," is to jokingly respond:
"Rule Number One: Panic!"
I do this to honor those in my midst who have already heeded the call to panic, even though they probably don't even know why. It's just what they do. It's always their first reaction to any situation.

If you think about it, this does actually make sense for many people. They don't have hope or trust in God, because they don't know Him. So, when something "breaks out," they panic because they have no one to turn to. It's just like people who trust in money. They have no hope, except in material things. So, when material things begin to disappear, or there is the chance that these material things will disappear, there is nothing, or no one, to turn to. This is the majority of people we see every day. They don't have Jesus, so how can they turn to someone they don't know?

That's why, when "the chips are down," they turn to us. They don't personally know the person in which our hope, trust, and future is in. But, they know us. And, when the "bottom drops out" in their lives, who do they turn to? They aren't willing-at that exact moment-to listen to Jesus, because they don't know Him. But, they know and trust us. Even if, when times are good, they would never associate with us. How often has God brought things into our lives in order to deepen our walk with Him, in order for us to know Him better?

Why do you think they always turn to us? Because God is using us to turn them to Him.

God is also taking the opportunity, in this poem, to give us, and our nation, the simple rule for success, the simple formula which our very survival may depend upon.

Panic, Prayer, Preparation

We're not panicking
We're praying
On our knees
We'll be staying

We don't need to panic
We need to pray
If we want
To see the light of day

Not panic
Preparation
That's what's kept safe
Our great nation

We need to prepare, not panic
We need to pray
To see another day

Why does all this matter
To you, and to me?
Because success is when preparation
Meets opportunity
The opportunity to pray
Should be seized without delay

So, prepare to pray
And, pray to prepare
Are you listening there?
That's the only way
In His loving arms
To stay

Let's all pray
Let's kneel in prayer
Be prepared
To meet Him right there

Over here
Over there
Prayer
Is the best way
To prepare

Rock Music
INTRODUCTION

Well, we've come to the part of our volume
where we feature "Rock Music!"
Now that we have your attention . . .

Perhaps no inanimate object is used more to
describe God, or Jesus, than "Rock."
I was looking for a way to introduce a couple of lines
that I had thought of, thinking of Jesus walking on the
water, with the phrase, "*This Rock don't sink!*"

I didn't know that Jesus would give me four pages of lines! But,
He did, and we feature them here. Again, here we have a story of
someone moved to repentance, and turning his life over to the Lord.

What made this work different is that the person was a
teenager, someone already heavily involved in the world, and
especially rock music. God incorporated several different
elements, including a couple of Gospel hymn standards
featuring the word "Rock," using the metaphor of drowning in
life's stormy ocean, and Jesus, walking on the water, coming
to rescue, save, and deliver a soul crying out to Him.

I am especially humbled by the fact that God
chose this work to proclaim Himself as
"*the first rock performer,*" as He "*took the rock and made it roll.*"

Rock Music

I was a teenager
I knew it all
Until I heard the Master's call

The night before, I was at a concert
The band was so loud
I felt like I was king of the world
But I was only part of a large crowd

The next day, I went to church
And that was where I heard
My first Rock music
And, not just the music
But the Word

*"Rock of Ages, cleft for me,
Let me hide myself in Thee"**

The Word was preached
Even the back row was reached
I heard about the Rock
And the Word He teached

I heard the music
About a man who walked on water
It was then I realized I was the clay
He was the Potter
All my life I had ran
Could it be?
That, for my life, there was a plan?

I thought of my life
Beginning to drown
My whole life was going down, down, down
But I heard of this Rock walking across the sea

On top of the water
I saw him reaching for,
Coming to me

Jesus, walking on top of the waves
I always thought I was so smart
But now I'm drowning
And Jesus saves
"Jesus, Jesus," I began to think
When this Rock went across the water
This Rock didn't sink

And, then it hit me
That, this Jesus, was God
What was I thinking?
Why was I sinking?
And, then, it hit me
Like a lightening rod

The night before
The world's songs I did sing
But, did they really mean anything?
Now, here was Jesus
And, He was the real King
King of the earth, King of everything
Calling to me, above the crowd
Speaking to me, in a voice I could feel
Speaking to me, in a voice so calm and still

Forget all I knew
The life I had known
All of the chances
I had so willingly blown
I saw, across the waters of my life
The weight of the burdens I bore
The tide could be turned
Jesus could save me
Before I crashed on the shore

I heard about Jesus
And, that, for even me, he would make room
I heard about Jesus, the cross
Forgiveness, and the empty tomb

I learned that God was the first Rock performer
That He sent Jesus to save my soul
I learned that after three days
God took the rock, and made it roll

My heart was sinking
My head was thinking
It was Sunday, so
I was hung over, don't you know
But, right now, I needed this drink
Living water, as I stood at the brink
Right now, I had to have this eternal drink
I needed this drink
From the Rock that don't sink

I drank and I drank
From the waters that flowed
I couldn't help but think
Of where I'd been just hours ago
At the foot of a stage
Screaming to an unknown band
Now, I cried from my knees
And reached out to the Savior's hand

He pulled me out of the depths
As He grasped my hand
Your sins are forgiven
Welcome to the Band

I thought of the song I had just heard
From a choir up ahead
Before the preaching of the Word
I thought how my head was no longer aching
From last night's rock band
For now, I had taken the Master's hand
As I led the chorus

"On Christ the solid rock I stand
All other ground is sinking sand
*All other ground is sinking sand"***
I couldn't help thinking
I'm no longer sinking
I'm no longer stinking
Because I held to the Savior's hand
I'm now part of the angel's brand
I'm now part of the Rock's band

*Rock of Ages: Written by Augustus Toplady
**My Hope is Built on Nothing Less: Written by Edward Mote/
Composed by William Bradbury

So Many Memories in so Short a Time
INTRODUCTION

This is a love story of what could be, what is hoped to be, and of what was meant to be.

I dedicate this to those who fell in love with their spouse the very first time they met, and are still in love . . . years later . . . and forever.

In this situation, the man and woman had "met" through mutual friends, where the friend had given the phone number of the lady to the man. The man had asked the mutual friend to call the lady, to make sure it was ok for him to call her. It was ok, and, after all, the lady was over 2,000 miles away, so it couldn't hurt; it was "safe" just to call her, right?

So, the man called the lady, and well . . . you can guess the rest. They became friends during these telephone conversations (which began in October), and stayed friends during the month of November. It just so happened that the mutual friend (who just happens to perform under a stage name) was the lead singer in a band (her husband played bass guitar in the band), and each year, they gave a special Christmas concert at a local venue. This was a big deal in the local area . . . a holiday event and concert "not to be missed."

Arrangements were made for the lady to fly into the city, just to meet the man . . . I mean . . . just for this concert event, and for no other reason . . . as it was such a special occasion . . . Well, the man had been speaking with the lady for two months, they had become close friends already, and this was his first opportunity to meet her, as he would be riding to the airport with their mutual friends, to meet the plane, as it arrived that Wednesday evening in mid-December . . .

I was standing there at the terminal, as the plane unloaded. I had never met anyone who was on the plane that day, but, when the lady (wearing a lavender top and brown winter coat with fleece edging) came through the tunnel, it was obvious that it was her. As flashbulbs popped, I remember hearing, "This is Carol . . ."

That was Wednesday night. The concert was Saturday. Before Carol left, I had spent two whole days with her. Before we left for the airport for her return trip on Sunday, I had proposed.

"So Many Memories in so Short a Time" was written about that first meeting at the airport. I realize now that the reason I remember those days so clearly, even these many years later, is because, for a few short days in December, time stood still.

So Many Memories in so Short a Time

So many memories
In so short a time
Is there any doubt
You were meant to be mine

Walking beside you in the airport
Just staring at your face
Listening to your voice
My heart began to race

Could it be, that this . . . you
You could be my true love
Things like this just don't happen
Unless they're sent from above

So many memories
In so short a time
Every step you took across the airport
Just seemed to rhyme

Beat, beat, beat
Went the sound of my heart
Am I watching forever
Ready to start?

As you reached for your luggage
I, too, reached down
As my hand touched yours
It wasn't just a suitcase I'd found

Up from the carousel
Our eyes just then met
I realized my future
Had arrived in that jet

Down the runway
Came my bride-to-be
I just never thought this . . . so wonderful
Could happen to me

It's no longer just an airport
But a shrine
To the time
Two lives met
And, now, forever, you're mine

So many memories
In so short a time

The Ark and the Covenant
INTRODUCTION

I often think of the story of Noah. We can get so easily discouraged when an individual, or a group, does not respond to our message. Or, we get overwhelmed with serving our congregation and community. Can you imagine what Noah must have gone through? At this time in history, he was the only preacher in the entire world. I also think of Noah as a Pastor. I try to remind people how important it is to be involved with a local congregation. The way I put it is that we all need to be under a Pastor's "umbrella;" under his care and prayer, which I see as a type of umbrella of protection. Noah had a small congregation, in fact, the only congregation in existence at the time, and, yes, they were all family. But, the umbrella example is proven, and his entire family was under it. Yes, we did all come from Adam, but we also all came from Noah . . . and his congregation.

Perhaps Noah's story is the greatest example of obedience in history. Remember that when God told him to build the ark, it had never rained before. It also would stand to reason-think about it-that there had never, ever been a cloudy day. No one had ever even seen a dark cloud in the sky. So, here he and his family were, building a huge ship . . . in the middle of a desert. You think you get made fun of? You think you get needled for your faith? When you stand on faith, against impossible odds . . . do people think you are crazy? It took 500 years to build the ark, and even when God shut the door, it still had never rained upon the earth.

Noah's story should greatly encourage us. That one man can make a difference for the entire world. It also tells me that, regardless of what sinful condition the world is in . . . no matter how bad the world situation is, God is always looking for a righteous man. It tells me that sometimes, you have to stand alone. You may be the only one . . . the only family . . . in the world . . . but God sees you, and that's all that matters. That's enough to save you, and your family. Maybe, even your world.

The Ark and the Covenant

God used a whole forest of green
To build a boat
The likes of which
Had never been seen

The ark
Was built to hold only eight
The cross was made
To carry the whole world's weight

The door was closed, water covered the earth
But in the ark, one family was safely shut in
The cross was made
To cover the whole world's sin

On top of the mountain
The ark would park
As Noah looked out
He didn't think of the flood
He thought of the ark

Eight people were all that were left
As years went by
The reality so stark
Noah chose not to remember
The flood
He chose to remember the ark

He remembered building a boat
In a desert dry as a bone
He remembered that sometimes
You have to stand alone

He remembered being the only one
Laboring all day in the hot sun
His family at his side
As whole cities would chide
He remembered, as his family flag he unfurled
He remembered that sometimes
You may be the only one
The only family in the world

He thought of a promise
Of a bow in the sky
A promise that still stands
For both you and for I

He remembered the covenant
He thought of it each time the rain would go away
He remembered that, often, the rainbow may go
But, the promise would always stay

He had no way of knowing
A new covenant would, one day, be in place
Written in the blood of God's son
A new covenant, supplied by God's grace

He thought of all the lumber, the nails
The wood and the boards, all the pitch and the tar
Covering his hands, his clothes, and his face
Noah had no way of knowing
That this was the only the first time
God would use wood to save the human race

He had no way of knowing
The world would become even darker with sin
That the whole world would need saving again
He had no way of knowing
The next time God chose to save you and me
He would only have to use one tree

Yes, just one tree
Would be all that was needed
Because of the One on the cross
God's plan totally succeeded

Yes, this new covenant
One of salvation
Is enough to save and to heal
Every one, every nation

God is still looking
For that one man, one family, to stand
In a world filled with darkness and sin
There's still room under this one tree
For your family, and for me
The cross of Calvary

The Bottomless Sea
INTRODUCTION

This is a praise psalm to God for His salvation and deliverance.
Because He will go to any depth to reach us, there is no place He won't or
can't go to deliver us, and there is no place that we can go where He isn't.

This was written from the passenger side of my father's truck, during
a trip from Georgia to Arkansas. As he drove, 45 miles an hour the
whole way, we hardly talked. Daddy didn't talk much as a rule, so I just
concentrated on the scenery, the continual stream of cars passing us, all
the while hoping he would pick up enough speed to change into fourth
gear. I remember thinking that at least we wouldn't have to slow down
if we had to take an exit off of the interstate.

The trip gave me ample time to just think about life, the past, and how
God had blessed me, promising me a glorious future under His care.
I remember that this was July, and as we drove into the hotel parking
lot, around 8:00PM, the sign had a temperature reading of 104 degrees.

It had been years since I had spent this much time with Daddy, and I
will always remember this time of being together. Of thinking what a
wonderful man he was, and among many other qualities, he was the
most honest man I have ever known. He is the only person I have ever
seen, who, when finding money (that wasn't his) in the change slot of a
vending machine, puts the money back into the machine. Because of the
way Daddy was, when I read the story of how Abraham Lincoln walked
several miles to return a borrowed book, I never doubted the story.

How often we forget how blessed we are, just to have parents like I've
had. To be raised in church, to have had a Godly upbringing, and then
when I went off into deep water, God rescuing me, bringing me up out
of the bottomless sea.

There is one thing, also, I'd like to mention about my father. It was
advice he gave me, during the darkest point in my life. Daddy wasn't

the type of father that you could just "talk to" about problems. Frankly, I was afraid to talk to him for most of my pre-adult life. However, as I look back, at the time I needed it most, he gave me a sentence . . . one sentence of advice and wisdom . . . wisdom that I have shared often, in the pages of this volume.

Without going into too much detail, it was a Sunday. I began that particular Sunday morning, after a sleepless Saturday night, by driving to a (supposed) close friend's home, and confronting the two who had "driven the stake through my heart." I guess there's no need to say more. I had only learned of the betrayal plot the night before. I left that house (or "den" as I would come to know it), and drove the 100 miles or so to my Mom and Dad's house. There was never a time in my life when I needed to see my parents more.
I explained to my Mom why I was alone . . . and then . . . the hard part. The hardest part, ever, was explaining anything to Daddy. I don't mean that as negative as it may seem. It was just so hard to talk to Daddy, especially when it was an emotionally-charged issue. I knew I had to tell him, somehow. He left the house to go out back to take care of the animals. I joined him, and as we walked across the yard, I feebly attempted to explain to Daddy what was going on, and why I had made the trip alone . . . why I was alone, period.

He looked at me, and then, stopped. It seemed the world stopped, as well. The look he gave me was one I'll never forget. It was a look of understanding and compassion. From Daddy! A man of so few words, he then spoke the words that will echo across the generations:

"Well, these things have a way of working out for the better."

When I was at the very bottom, both my father and Jesus were there for me.

The Bottomless Sea

Oh my God!
How you have delivered me!
From the depths of
The bottomless sea

I fell and I fell
And you were there
To show me again
How much you care

Before I could
Drop far out of sight
You held me up
And held me so tight

As deeper, yet deeper
I went
The deeper I'd go
The further you bent

There is no question or doubt
For now I know
To show
How you love me
There's no place
You wouldn't go

For you are my God
My Lord and my Savior
Who loves me in spite
Of my awful, sinful behavior

Thank you, God
For saving me
For keeping me
Out of the bottomless sea

The Eagle Still Flies
INTRODUCTION

*The fabric of America is woven with the threads of time
and patriotism. The fabric can be torn, or burned. But,
the pattern that this cloth is made from is courage."
Richard.Vincent.Rose.*
Originally written on the back of a Wal-Mart Receipt

To fully appreciate the poem, we must go back to the days and months immediately following the events of September 11, 2001. "The Eagle Still Flies" captures the mindset of what Americans, and our friends all over the word, had at that exact moment in time.

Today, I teach students who weren't even born in 2001. Just as we did in school, as we learned about Pearl Harbor and World War II, events which happened before we were born. What stood out then, and now, is the patriotism which these tragic events would birth across the United States, and the world. As a fan of "Old Time Radio," I have radio programs from that era which, frankly, would not even be allowed to be broadcast on the airwaves today.

America was attacked. By an enemy who wished to destroy us, and especially, our way of life.
What the enemy did not realize, just as in World War II, was that what was called "a sleeping giant" in the 1940's, may have been sleeping, but it was still very much alive.

As I write this, we are still at war. Daniel Webster said that "God grants liberty only to those who love it, and are always ready to guard and defend it." It simply can't be overstated that freedom is not free, nor ever has been. One of my favorite quotes regarding military service is this: "If you don't stand behind our troops, you are welcome to stand in front of them."

Years ago, I had the distinct privilege of being elected to be the first vice-president of a regional writers club. The members consisted of individuals who had lived in all parts of the world. At least one of the members did not have a particularly positive view of the United States. After I had shared what was then a newly written "The Eagle Still Flies," he offered a rebuttal of sorts, and called me a "Patriot." His tone carried the same negative tone of what it must have sounded like when people began to call the early Disciples of Christ a "Christian." Well, I am today, as I was that day, proud to carry the banner of "Patriot," and be associated with others who have carried that same banner. Just as I am proud to carry the banner of Christ, and be associated with those who have, and still, carry His banner.

Original Spoken Introduction to "The Eagle Still Flies"

I'd like to share with you the original introduction, which I would dramatically read before the poem. Keep in mind that this was first presented while the memories of the terrorist attacks on our country were still fresh in our minds. This is the original copy transcript:

2 Corinthians 3:17 says that where the spirit of the Lord is, there is liberty. When I see the word, "liberty" or "freedom" I see Jesus' name written all over it.
Thomas Paine said, in 1776, that "The cause of America is, in a great measure, the cause of all mankind."

On September 11, 2001, evil called . . .
Interesting . . . 911 . . .
And, an entire nation answered.

We went from a nation known for rock 'n roll
To take pride in Plymouth Rock, and "Let's roll!"

We went from a place know as "Ground Zero"
To a place known as "Ground Hero."

Let the word go forth
Through time and space
The United States of America is the center of peace and strength
Tranquility base is here
The eagle has landed
And the eagle still flies
Under star-spangled skies

And, now . . .
A new patriotic poem for America . . .
"The Eagle Still Flies (Under Star-Spangled Skies) . . ."

The Eagle Still Flies
A New Anthem for America

The sun came up this morning
Over a land still brave and free
Its borders still strong and standing
Against all tyranny

It seems just yesterday, I remember so well
As the morning dew slept on the towers that fell
The skies were so clear, the sunlight so bright
But evil's conscience couldn't sleep
And was awake through the night

Everyone can recall when they first heard the news
No one was sure how much more we would lose
Then, through the ashes, the smoke, and the flame
We realized this country would never be the same

The towers left standing
Are the towers within
The twin towers of liberty and freedom, my friend
Perched on top of these towers, the eagle will rise
To bring peace and justice to the world's crying eyes

And the eagle still flies
Under star-spangled skies
And we still trust in God
But we won't spare the rod
And we still say the pledge
Faith and courage
Give us the edge
And the eagle will soar
'Cause we're free evermore
From the hills to the shore
Yes! We're free evermore

The eagle still flies under star-spangled skies
And our hope never dies
'Cause the eagle still flies
Nations will rise
Buildings will fall
But there's still one nation standing
That will answer the call
And we won't run and hide
In our flag we still take pride
'Cause freedom will win
Liberty we'll defend

Through the smoke, through the fire
The wings of justice fly higher
Over canyon and tundra and treetops and sand
The fires of freedom's victory have been fanned

From the streets on our soil
To lands across the sea
On freedom's wings we will ride
For the whole world to see
The strength, the power, of liberty

And the eagle still flies
Under star-spangled skies
And we still trust in God
But we won't spare the rod
And we still say the pledge
Faith and courage give us the edge

And the eagle will soar
'Cause we're free evermore
From the hills to the shore
Yes! We're free evermore

The eagle still flies
Under star-spangled skies
And our hope never dies
'Cause the eagle still flies

The Kind of Guys I Want to Be
INTRODUCTION

On our Pastor Appreciation Blog, we featured a set of pictures, taken over time and in different circumstances, featuring soldiers who were praying, or were rescuing children. All of the pictures were taken from soldiers serving in Iraq or Afghanistan. I had received the pictures from several different friends, and I had stored them, hoping to use them some day.

I carefully studied the pictures, many of which fell into the category of "if that don't break it, you don't have one." Suddenly, God gave me the words, as I realized, that "these are the kind of guys I want to be." Yes, the word "guys" here is generic, as the photographs featured both men and women soldiers. So, "from out of nowhere," I featured parts of the poem between the photographs. The response was overwhelming.

There is an old saying that "there are no atheists in foxholes." How often I have prayed that I am not going to wait until I get into a "foxhole;" I'm going to pray right now. I need God *before* I get into trouble. Maybe if I would pray more . . . I wouldn't have to worry about trouble so much. I also like to pray that I am bowing at the feet of Jesus right now, and declare Him as Lord . . . before that time comes when everyone will. Same thing: If I do that right now, I won't have to worry about that later time when everyone will bow and declare . . .

Soldiers that pray . . . these are the kind of guys I want to see . . . these are the kind of guys I want to be. And, yes, guys who will pray are the kind of guys I want living next to me. You can talk about government or organizations . . . but, guys that will pray are the kind of guys who represent me, and represent those who are the closest to me.

The Kind of Guys I Want to Be

I came across a picture of some soldiers
They were in a circle, in uniform
They were joined in prayer
Now, I know what some soldiers
Are doing over there

You see, I am a soldier, too
A different battle I fight
But, it's because of those soldiers
That I can sleep safely at night

You ask what this means
What does this have to do with you?
Well, it's because of those soldiers
That you can sleep safely, too

I look again at the picture, the circle of prayer
And I begin to realize
What kind of heroes they are
And, that, these are the kind of guys:

I want praying for me
I want praying for my country
These are the kind of guys
I want fighting for me
I want fighting for my country
These are the kind of guys
I want representing me
I want representing my country

These are the kind of guys
I want to see
These are the kind of guys
I want my country to see
These are the kind of guys

I want the world to see
These are the kind of guys
That I want God to see
God has already seen them
And, He has heard their prayer
I, now, have seen them
I can't help but to stare
And, to wonder
Would I pray like that
If I was over there?

I look at the picture, and I see
What they see
Liberty
I look at the picture, and I know
What they know
Freedom
What they know
It will grow
That's what I know

These are the kind of guys
I want to see on the battlefield
Or, where ever they may roam
These are the kind of guys
I want to see
I want to see come home

These are the kind of guys I want to see
As neighbors, living next to me
These are the kind of guys I want to see
In my neighborhood
As friends
Standing next to me

These are the kind of guys
I want to see
These are the kind of guys

Who represent me
These are the kind of guys
I want the world to see
These are the kind of guys
That I want to be
These are the kind of guys
I want to see
These are the kind of guys
Who know about liberty

These are the kind of guys
Who aren't just bums
These are the kind of guys
Who know about freedom
And, from where it comes

These are the kind of guys
We need more of
These are the kind of guys
Who bow to look above
These are the kind of guys
I want to see
These are the kind of guys
That I want to be

If they knew who I was
While on bended knee
I would hope that these soldiers
Would be praying for me

I want to be a warrior
A warrior in prayer
Lord, help me to pray here
Like they do over there

We can learn a lot from a soldier who will pray
He doesn't know if he'll live another day
One thing is true
Neither do you

The Mold of Gold
INTRODUCTION

Perhaps I heard the old saying that "When God made you, He threw away the mold." Which, if you think about it, is one of those sayings which doesn't make sense. If we really believe that God created each of us to be different, that we are all an individual creation, then there really is no mold, is there?

I am amazed, and can't comprehend, how each snowflake can be different. There are no two snowflakes exactly alike. Yet, when someone acts differently from us, we are surprised.
This is the story of someone who met someone . . . their perfect match. The one they had been looking for their entire life.

It is also a story to encourage you. That God has a plan, and He has the perfect "someone," which He created just for you. You just haven't met them yet. It's true: God has created someone for everyone. Even you.

The reason I know is, well, because I know. I went through a long period of time when I really believed that it just wasn't meant for me to be married. I thought of all kind of examples . . . yes, even Biblical examples. When I would travel from town to town, every night visiting a different grocery store for supper (I always used the microwave in the hotel room), I would be so glad I wasn't married. It seemed that every evening, I would be walking the grocery aisles, and there would always be that one man, shopping with his wife . . . you know the one . . . you knew that the last place on earth he wanted to be was there . . . even from several aisles away, you could hear them arguing. It didn't matter what town, or what grocery store I was in, that same guy was always there.

After leaving the grocery store, I used to thank God every night that I wasn't married. God knew that's the way I felt when, one evening, I had come home early, on a Thursday. I never came in on a Thursday! I was tired, so I went to the closest grocery store, in order to just run in and get out. It was a grocery store that I never went to, because I had a bad experience there, running into someone I never wanted to see again, and didn't want to take the chance again. I was almost out the door, when I heard a voice calling me, a lady in line at another register, who recognized me as I walked by on the way out . . . It was a lady, now a dear friend, whom I had not seen in years . . . who caught me just in time to tell me of a friend she had, in Connecticut . . . who would be perfect for me . . .

The Mold of Gold

When God made you
He didn't throw away the mold
He gave it to me
And, my soul has been looking for the perfect fit
Ever since

There were others, who didn't fit
And, just when I threw up my arms
Sat down, and quit

See . . . it wasn't my mold they didn't fit
It was yours!
I was trying to get them
To fit your mold
The Mold of Gold

There was no way they could fit
No way they should

The reason I knew
That you were the one
The reason I knew that you were the one?
Remember, I've been looking at your mold
The Mold of Gold
All of my life
Since time had begun

The one that would fit
You are the one
The one planned from above
To be my wife
That is why I can say
From my heart and soul
When I met you
It wasn't that I was looking
It was that I knew
When to stop looking

A form? A mold?
This isn't for someone to "get"
Anyone can see, from looking at you
That you do fit

See, I didn't make the mold
I didn't make the one that fit
But I can make this promise:
This is the one thing in my whole, entire life
That I will not quit

From before
From days of old
You are the one
Of which I was told
Because you are the one
The one made to fit
The Mold of Gold

There Was a Man Who Took a Stand
INTRODUCTION

I wanted to write something to honor those who are active in the children's ministry, as that is a church ministry I have personally been involved in.

I remember a Pastor saying that when we line up in Heaven to receive our reward, the nursery workers and those from Kid's Church will be first in line. He was trying to explain how difficult it is to work in these areas, how much of a sacrifice it is, and how important these ministries are. I have known many parents who have visited a church, and the first room they want to see is either the nursery, or Kid's Church. It didn't matter how awesome the "big church" (I use this term to let you know I really was involved in Children's ministry) was, how powerful God may be moving within the sanctuary . . . if they didn't like the nursery, or the children's ministry, they wouldn't be back.

This is a children's singing verse we wrote, sung to the tune of the traditional song, "There was a farmer who had a dog, and Bingo was his name-o."

Of course, we started with "JESUS," and added "MOSES" to the rhyme. The beautiful thing about this verse is that you can use almost any name, as you teach the heroes of the Bible. Another beautiful thing about this verse is that you can add names of those heroes you know today, from your own life and experience. It is natural to add names which have five letters, such as Jesus, Moses, Peter, James, etc. However, you can easily add a four letter name, just by extending the 3rd letter, as you see in the third example verse, using the name "Paul." I've added a fourth example, to use for names with six letters in their name, such as "Martin," or, perhaps "Nelson." This just takes a faster clap count, using two groups of three claps, and it works out great!

This is a wonderful, fun way to teach, and honor those from our past, and present, whom we admire for "taking a stand." To encourage all of us, we have included a fifth example, which begins with "God needs a man to take a stand, and _____ is his name-o." Here, you just add someone who is present in the group, to encourage them to "take a stand."

There Was a Man Who Took a Stand
(Traditional Rhyme)

Example Verse 1:
There was a man who took a stand,
And Jesus was his name-o.
J-E-S-U-S
J-E-S-U-S
J-E-S-U-S
And Jesus was his name-o.

There was a man who took a stand,
And Jesus was his name-o.
(clap)-E-S-U-S
(clap)-E-S-U-S
(clap)-E-S-U-S
And Jesus was his name-o.

There was a man who took a stand,
And Jesus was his name-o.
(clap)-(clap)-S-U-S
(clap)-(clap)-S-U-S
(clap)-(clap)-S-U-S
And Jesus was his name-o.

There was a man who took a stand,
And Jesus was his name-o.
(clap)-(clap)-(clap)-U-S
(clap)-(clap)-(clap)-U-S
(clap)-(clap)-(clap)-U-S
And Jesus was his name-o.

There was a man who took a stand,
And Jesus was his name-o.
(clap)-(clap)-(clap)-(clap)-S
(clap)-(clap)-(clap)-(clap)-S
(clap)-(clap)-(clap)-(clap)-S
And Jesus was his name-o.

There was a man who took a stand,
And Jesus was his name-o.
(clap)-(clap)-(clap)-(clap)-(clap)
(clap)-(clap)-(clap)-(clap)-(clap)
(clap)-(clap)-(clap)-(clap)-(clap)
And Jesus was his name-o.

Example Verse 2:
There was a man who took a stand,
And Moses was his name-o.
M-O-S-E-S
M-O-S-E-S
M-O-S-E-S
And Moses was his name-o.

There was a man who took a stand,
And Moses was his name-o.
(clap)-O-S-E-S
(clap)-O-S-E-S
(clap)-O-S-E-S
And Moses was his name-o.

There was a man who took a stand,
And Moses was his name-o.
(clap)-(clap)-S-E-S
(clap)-(clap)-S-E-S
(clap)-(clap)-S-E-S
And Moses was his name-o.

There was a man who took a stand,
And Moses was his name-o.
(clap)-(clap)-(clap)-E-S
(clap)-(clap)-(clap)-E-S
(clap)-(clap)-(clap)-E-S
And Moses was his name-o.

There was a man who took a stand,
And Moses was his name-o.
(clap)-(clap)-(clap)-(clap)-S
(clap)-(clap)-(clap)-(clap)-S
(clap)-(clap)-(clap)-(clap)-S
And Moses was his name-o.

There was a man who took a stand,
And Moses was his name-o.
(clap)-(clap)-(clap)-(clap)-(clap)
(clap)-(clap)-(clap)-(clap)-(clap)
(clap)-(clap)-(clap)-(clap)-(clap)
And Moses was his name-o.

Example Verse 3:
There was a man who took a stand,
And Paul was his name-o.
P-A-U-U-L
P-A-U-U-L
P-A-U-U-L
And Paul was his name-o.

There was a man who took a stand,
And Paul was his name-o.
(clap)-A-U-U-L
(clap)-A-U-U-L
(clap)-A-U-U-L
And Paul was his name-o.

There was a man who took a stand,
And Paul was his name-o.
(clap)-(clap)-U-U-L
(clap)-(clap)-U-U-L
(clap)-(clap)-U-U-L
And Paul was his name-o.

There was a man who took a stand,
And Paul was his name-o.
(clap)-(clap)-(clap)-U-L
(clap)-(clap)-(clap)-U-L
(clap)-(clap)-(clap)-U-L
And Paul was his name-o.

There was a man who took a stand,
And Paul was his name-o.
(clap)-(clap)-(clap)-(clap)-L
(clap)-(clap)-(clap)-(clap)-L
(clap)-(clap)-(clap)-(clap)-L
And Paul was his name-o.

There was a man who took a stand,
And Paul was his name-o.
(clap)-(clap)-(clap)-(clap)-(clap)
(clap)-(clap)-(clap)-(clap)-(clap)
(clap)-(clap)-(clap)-(clap)-(clap)
And Paul was his name-o.

Example Verse 4:
There was a man who took a stand,
And Martin was his name-o.
MAR-T I N
MAR-T I N
MAR-T I N
And Martin was his name-o.

There was a man who took a stand,
And Martin was his name-o.
(clap)-A-R-T-I-N
(clap)-A-R-T-I-N
(clap)-A-R-T-I-N
And Martin was his name-o.

There was a man who took a stand,
And Martin was his name-o.
(clap)-(clap)-R-T-I-N
(clap)-(clap)-R-T-I-N
(clap)-(clap)-R-T-I-N
And Martin was his name-o.

There was a man who took a stand,
And Martin was his name-o.
(clap)-(clap)-(clap)- T-I-N
(clap)-(clap)-(clap)- T-I-N
(clap)-(clap)-(clap)- T-I-N
And Martin was his name-o.

There was a man who took a stand,
And Martin was his name-o.
(clap)-(clap)-(clap)-(clap)- I-N
(clap)-(clap)-(clap)-(clap)- I-N
(clap)-(clap)-(clap)-(clap)- I-N
And Martin was his name-o.

There was a man who took a stand,
And Martin was his name-o.
(clap)-(clap)-(clap)-(clap)-(clap)-N
(clap)-(clap)-(clap)-(clap)-(clap)-N
(clap)-(clap)-(clap)-(clap)-(clap)-N
And Martin was his name-o.

There was a man who took a stand,
And Martin was his name-o.
(clap)-(clap)-(clap)-(clap)-(clap)- (clap)
(clap)-(clap)-(clap)-(clap)-(clap)- (clap)
(clap)-(clap)-(clap)-(clap)-(clap)- (clap)
And Martin was his name-o.

Example Verse 5:
God needs a man to take a stand
And _____ is his name-o.
JUST FILL IN THE NAME AND SING THE SONG!!!

The State of Missing You
INTRODUCTION

So often, we hear those sad old songs about being lonely, etc. I know; I've written them, too.

There are many times when we must legitimately be away from home on business . . . even evangelists and missionaries must, often, travel alone. Isn't it funny how we write stories or songs of how *we* feel, and that's ok. Then, we speak of evangelists or missionaries, Pastors or preachers, and, we somehow, put them in a different category. Like they aren't human, or have the same feelings we have. Like, it's not ok for them to be in love with their wife, or families, just like they are in love with Jesus.

I wrote of this earlier, and the case remains: It's ok . . . even if you are a Christian . . . even if you are a Pastor . . . even if you are an evangelist . . . even if you are a missionary . . . to love your wife, and to miss her. It's ok to love your family, and to miss them. It's even ok to miss your friends, or your home!

What do you mean, what about professional athletes, or those we call "celebrities?" I think we put the wrong people on the wrong pedestals, for the wrong reasons. God made us all human, with the same feelings. It is us who are "respecter of persons," not Him. I don't love my wife, family, or Jesus any less because I am not in a particular field, vocation, or profession . . . we will all be judged the same.

Another reason I wrote this was that I really loved the idea behind the title. It speaks of being in a crowd, and being alone, because "you" aren't there. There are people traveling who will read this, regardless of their reason for traveling, and they will understand this, and it will bless them. That is what my writing is all about. I've been there, I know how you feel, and it feels like this . . .

In my hotel, I always had the room telephone and a cell phone. I know what it's like to be in a strange hotel, miles from anyone you know, and be totally alone. There is no one to call, and there is no one who will be calling you. That's why I really appreciated the line,

"My room has two phones, which only makes me twice as lonely."

The State of Missing You

Different day
Different road
Different hotel
Same State
The State of Missing You

I love you!
I miss you!
I need you!
Etc!

Well, here I am in North Carolina
And, Hey!
It's just like being home!!!

That's right
Just like home
I'm alone
And, without you

Hey! Just like home!
All I want
Is you beside me

Every State I'm in
I'm in the same State
The State of missing you
The State of loving you
The State of needing you

My room has two phones
Which only makes me
Twice as lonely
That's two phones
Which won't ring
With the sound of your voice

Different day-I love you!
Different road-I miss you!
Different hotel-I need you

Same State
The State of Missing You

The Sweetest Sound I've Ever Heard
INTRODUCTION

This is a poem I wrote in praise to God for how much He had blessed me with Carol and our life together.

Only a few days before, Carol had accepted Jesus as her Savior, giving her life over to Him. It had happened at home, just me and her, and it happened right in the center of our kitchen. Only a few months before, I had proposed to Carol, just before she flew back home to Connecticut, in the center of my kitchen, back in Georgia.

I thought about how God had changed everything in our lives. How big a change in Carol's life Jesus had already made. To this day, Carol continues to be the most influential Christian example in my life.

This is the poem which I wrote while I sat at the wrong restaurant, on the only thing I could find to write on, an old grocery list.

I have read this poem, and told the story behind it to many an audience. It always gets a marvelous reaction. I am never totally sure they believe the story of actually writing this on an old grocery list . . . until I raise up the grocery list, with the words scribbled down, among the "toilet paper" and "vegetables," for all to see.

I encourage you to read the story behind the poem, to be blessed . . . and to not give up hope!

The Sweetest Sound I've Ever Heard

We've traveled far
We've traveled wide
And always, you were by my side
Every concert, symphony, every band
Sounds so sweet as if from God's own hand

I've heard the ocean's surf
A baby's cries after birth
Seen the bluest skies above
Felt the deepest kind of love
Heard every kind of music
Seen every kind of show
But, the sweetest sound I've ever heard
I heard not so long ago

When we were first married
We chose to read from the Bible every day
And I prayed that God's Word would take hold
Somewhere along the way
But, where to start?
At what book to begin?
She wanted to learn it all
From the beginning until the end

I waited with hope
As each night's reading would arrive
I secretly prayed for me to get out of the way
And let God's Word come alive
It was then that I would hear
The most beautiful sound
To ever penetrate my ear

The Bible was opened
Pages were searched up and down
Then my heart would leap

As I would hear that sound
The most beautiful sound
My soul had ever heard
Yes, the sound
The sound of my wife reading God's Word

She would look up from the Scriptures
When a question was raised
She had so many questions
I would say to myself, "God be praised!"

How powerful, you ask
Is God's holy Word?
Can it really unlock your chains
And make you as free as a bird?
Well, I can only report
What I've seen and heard
The result of what happened
When my wife read God's Word

She started reading at creation
And never got bored
By the time we got to Genesis 14
She had given her heart to the Lord

You see, Jesus would burst forth from the pages
Old Testament, or New
He's still the Rock of Ages

So, for all the world's noise
I give it not a look
What sets my soul afire is her
Reading from that Book
Yes, the sweetest sound
That I've ever heard
Is the sound of my wife's voice
Reading God's Word

"We"
INTRODUCTION

Most of the publicity surrounding my writing comes from those works which are meant for a public forum, but, there are a couple of works which are meant for a more private audience.

This would be one. It focuses on the feeling that I hope we all feel one day, truly the most indescribable feeling of all, between two people. Not only do they really feel this way, but, they both know that God brought them together. I know that people who don't really know God toss about the old "God brought us together" theme, just like people who don't really know Him bring His name up a lot in conversation.

This is another "you know what I mean" writing, where there is no doubt this is exactly the way you feel. I used to work with a lady who could not speak good English . . . it was because of her that God gave me the saying, *Compassion doesn't have an accent.* This is about the language of the eyes and heart . . . the two major languages spoken by those in love.

Haven't we already discussed the fact that it's ok to love your wife? Well, before she was your wife, she was your girlfriend or fiancée, right? I have written about loving your wife, but this is one just for that time between when she said "yes," and when you "walked down the aisle." Yes, it's ok to love them during that time, too! In fact, wouldn't you agree, that from a "walking on air" standpoint, this is one of the greatest times of your life? This poem speaks of the language of love, which has nothing to do with words.

We have written how these "love messages" are metaphoric in nature, symbolizing Christ's love for us, and our love for Him. The real amazement is not that we love Jesus . . . look what He's done for us . . . The really amazing thing is that He loves us!

And, so it is with my wife, or in your situation, your wife. In my case, it's not amazing that I would love Carol. She is the most wonderful person I have ever known. Besides my mother, she is the most Christ-like example I have ever known. Every description of her includes the phrase that "she is the most genuinely nice person I have ever met." She is my biggest fan. Ok, she's beautiful, too! So, just like in the case with Jesus . . . the amazing thing is not that I would love her . . . it's the fact that she loves me!

"We"

I know now that God
Never intended it to be
Just "Me"
I know now that God had a plan
A plan for it to be
"We"

It is no more "Me"
From now on
It is
"We"

I just can't forget the way
That you said, "Yes!"
Before you, love was so foreign
I must confess
For me, not at 40
But, life began
When you said, "Yes!"

When you said
"Yes, I will be your bride,"
And you promised
To always be by my side
No more alone I would ever be
Because by my side you will forever be

In any language
Your eyes speak with love
You heart translates
What was written above

The road planned for us
Only wide enough for two
Every tick of the clock
Brings me one second closer to you

Any country, any nation
Our love would stand out
From London to Paris
They know that this is what love is all about

In English, your "Yes!"
Meant we'll always be
Funny, how in France
"Yes" means "Oui"

Why, Jesus, Why
INTRODUCTION

It was always in the back of my mind to write this. It's one of those things that you know you are supposed to write, that you should write, but . . .

God gave me the words to "Why, Pastor, Why," and He would have to give me the words to "Why, Jesus, Why." And, because of the perceived "pressure" to write this, I just never got the words, or, really, inclination or call, to write this.

You may be thinking: If you are writing the words to why Jesus saved you . . . why Jesus delivered you . . . why Jesus called you . . . why would you need a "special" inspiration to write this? Couldn't you just write down "Why" Jesus did this for you?

Good questions! But, the reason why I failed at the words is because I am still in awe of why Jesus saved and chose me. In my heart of hearts, I know that I'm not worth it, for the King of Glory to even "be seen with me," let alone be associated with me. I don't know "why" he would use me. If you are a Christian, truly in love with Jesus, you will know exactly what I mean. We've done nothing to deserve His love, nor can we ever be "good enough" to deserve anything He can give us.

However, here is the real reason I hadn't written a work with the title, "Why, Jesus, Why:" It's because it was Him who gave me the first one . . . I just held the pen, remember? In order to write this one, the same circumstances would have to apply. Until He, personally, gave me the words, it just wasn't going to happen, and I knew it.

Well, in church one Sunday morning, sixteen years after "Why, Pastor, Why," Jesus began dealing with me about the words to "Why, Jesus, Why." I wrote the first lines on the back of the church program, in the "Sermon Notes" section . . .

It describes, perfectly, where I was, and where He was . . . the whole time . . . It wasn't about me, it was about all of us . . . not those behind the pulpit, but those who are in front of it . . .

Why, Jesus, Why

Why, Jesus, why
Would you choose me?
Why would you call me out
To fulfill your ministry?

Not behind a pulpit
Or podium stand
Just walk every day
Holding to Your hand

For so long
From you
I ran
I refused to grasp your message
Or your nail-scarred hand
For so long, seems my whole life through
I've spent just running
Running from you

Day after day
I thought I was running
From you
I never realized, the whole time
With every step
I was running
Toward you

I wondered why, Jesus why
Sometimes, you didn't pursue
It's because each step I took
Brought me one step closer to you

Why, Jesus why
Didn't I
Realize I
Was the one running
You were the one standing
Waiting for me
Waiting for me
Now I see
You were just waiting
Waiting for me

Why, Pastor, Why
INTRODUCTION

"The reason, Pastor, that you mean so much to me
Is that when I look at you
It's Jesus that I see"

"Why, Pastor, Why" is a poem specifically purposed to uplift and encourage Pastors. While it is written to show love and appreciation, it also answers the basic question every Pastor must address-both in times of joy and in those moments of despair and discouragement:

"Why has God chosen me for this office?"

During his Sunday night sermon, "Pastor Dan" used himself as an example to illustrate the awesome grace and mercy of God. He humbly acknowledged he did not know, nor could he understand, why God had reached down to save him, or why God had entrusted him with the anointed task of ministry.

Later that night, as I pondered my Pastor's "Why?" the Lord answered the question for me, giving me the poem, "Why, Pastor, Why." He further revealed that His answer applied not only to Pastor Dan, but to all Pastors. Then, He directed me to reach all Pastors with this simple message.

"The office of Pastor is the highest office in the land.
For, the people choose the president. God chooses the Pastor."

Many times, I have heard the startling statistics of the number of Pastors who are leaving the ministry. We as Christians can forget how we were, before the Lord "called us out." We forget how much He has done for us, and how many lives we have affected through our faith. How much greater the burden must be for these men and women who devote their lives to the Gospel. They must "keep on keeping on!" Not just for themselves, but for the lives they touch. The call is not just for them, but for their flock.

I firmly believe that God wishes to give this message of encouragement to all pastors, and their congregations, world-wide.

"The greatest gift God gives the local church is their Pastor."

Why, Pastor, Why

As I see you standing there behind the pulpit
Reading from God's Word
I think back to all those wonderful, blessed sermons
From you that I've heard
No, there's no secret why God brought you out
Oh! The many times your joy has made me shout!
You see, Pastor, there was a reason that God saved your soul
Because He knew that serving Him with all your heart
Would be your life's goal
You see, Pastor, there was a reason that it was you
That God chose
Not your good looks, perfect hair, and stylish clothes
No, Pastor, the reason that God reached down His hand and saved you
Let there be no doubt!
The reason God chose you
Is because He knew
How you would turn out!
The reason, Pastor, that you mean so much to me
Is that when I look at you
It's Jesus that I see
For in your footsteps I so gratefully trod
Because I know that in following you
I am following God

Why, Pastor, Why (The Song)
INTRODUCTION

This song represents the Pastor who is *"there, with me and Jesus, standing so tall . . . Whose eyes, ears, and heart are focused on where he is needed most."*

Even as God had given me the poem, "Why, Pastor, Why," He would give me the words to a song which would honor Pastors.

This is another work which took many years to complete. I had the beginning of the song, which began with *"At the bedside of my sister, so weak and so frail,"* in my mind for several years, before God gave me the rest. I vividly remember being in this same situation, and, at the time needed most, the Pastor would reach out for the one who needed help the most.

It has to do with the Pastor being guided to the place "where he was needed most," which is, so often, not the place where the event is happening, but to the place where the effects of that happening will be felt the most.

This song took fifteen years to complete, and takes us to a place where the Pastor's words, prayers, and actions are felt by all in attendance. We have all been there. When the Pastor arrives, his purpose is not just for one . . . his calling is for all . . . For, all will need him, will depend upon him, will trust him, will listen to him, and will look to him . . .

I'd like to dedicate this song to those Pastors whom I have personally known, and to those whom you have personally known, which fulfill the words to both the poem and song "Why, Pastor, Why."

"Pastor, next to Jesus, you are the finest man I've ever known.
For, when I think of you, that is where I always see you . . . Next to Jesus."
R.V.R.

Why, Pastor, Why
(The Song)

I know why, Pastor, why
That God chose you
It is why, Pastor, why
I can make it through

When my whole world around me
Is fallen and gone
When the dust has all settled
As I stand against the wall
You are there, with me and Jesus
Standing so tall

At the bedside of my sister
So weak and so frail
The family knew at any moment
Her breathing could fail
I looked at her husband
Through tears in my eyes
The pain, the loss, the heartache
He could not disguise

Then, I remembered a prayer
I heard just moments before
From a voice so reassuring, so strong
So great a compassion
It seemed my burden he bore
His prayer filled the whole house
With such overwhelming peace
Because we knew that his prayer
Had reached
All the way to the mercy seat

I knew why, Pastor, why
That God chose you
It was why, Pastor, why
I could make it through

When my whole world around me
Was fallen and gone
When the dust had all settled
As I stood against the wall
You were there, with me and Jesus
Standing so tall

As the angels made
One last circle of the house
In the stillness I glimpsed
My best friend, my sister's spouse
As my brother-in-law collapsed
From the weight of his loss
I saw two hands, catch him
From nowhere, they seemed
In the shape of a cross

As the rest of the family had gathered
For the last breath
From my sister's bed post
My Pastor's eyes had been focused
On where he was needed most

He knew why, Pastor, why
That God had chosen you
It was why, Pastor, why
That he could make it through

When his whole world around him
Was fallen and gone
When the dust had all settled
As he stood against the wall
You were there, with him and Jesus
Standing so tall

God sent an under-shepherd
To take care of his flock
Someone to help us
During times of joy, pain
And, sometimes, great shock

A man that would give his all
To each one of us
Through the long days
And short nights
He would not complain or fuss

A man that that is there
To help see us all through
Because, for him
Heaven won't be the same
Unless you
Are there too

Now, I know why, Pastor, why
That God chose you
It is why, Pastor, why
I can make it through

When my whole world around me
Is fallen and gone
When the dust has all settled
As I stand against the wall
You are there, with me and Jesus
Standing so tall

You're My Yuletide Carol
INTRODUCTION

People find it hard to believe, but it's true: I wrote this Christmas song before I had ever met Carol. I had spoken with her often on the telephone, but we had never met. The first time we met was at Atlanta Hartsfield Airport, when she was visiting Georgia to attend a concert given every year by mutual friends of ours. I've often written of how "I just knew" that Carol was the one I was to spend the rest of my life with.

Carol arrived on a Wednesday night, and the concert was Saturday. She helped me make changes to the work, and our friends hurriedly put the music together, and played this as a special song at the concert. I've always envisioned this as a new Christmas classic, sung by someone like Tony Bennett.

I got the idea a few days before Christmas, as I was getting ready for Carol's visit. I was playing a favorite Christmas album (yes, I still play albums), and, from out of nowhere, the phrase "Yuletide Carols" just seemed to freeze in mid-air. So, I grabbed it, and wrote this in advance of Carol's visit.

I was asked to include the song in this volume, and I hope it shows some variety in my work. I am grateful for the opportunity to share this song with you. I hope you enjoy it. And, again, I remind you that it's ok to love your wife! And, to say you do.

You're My Yuletide Carol
(Full Version)

You're my Yuletide Carol
And I love you so
You're my Yuletide Carol
I just want you to know

My Christmas wish comes true
As your plane touches down
I can't wait, my dear
To show you the town
You've been so long in the frozen north
The stairs unfold as my holiday bursts forth

And you're my Yuletide Carol
And I love you so
You're my Yuletide Carol
And my heart's all aglow

As I catch my first glimpse of you
At the gate
I know in an instant
That it was worth the wait
As your smile melted the icicles
From around my heart
I just can't wait
For my holidays to start

My hopes and my dreams
Won't be dashed through the snow
Cause you're my Yuletide Carol
And I love you so

The nights are no more silent
My heart's all aglow
And you're my Yuletide Carol
And you're as lovely as a bow

Oh! The sights that we will see
All over Christmas town
I'm so thankful that in your arms
This Yuletide spirit I've found
Your love is enough
To last the year round

So much to see
So much to do
A few days left
And the holidays are through
You're my Yuletide Carol
And I love you so
So soon you'll be gone
Just like the snow

Christmas bells are all ringing
And the skies are so clear
A warm fire is burning
As I hold you near
The light in your eyes sparkle
Like the new fallen snow
The season soon over
Where, oh where, did it go?

And you're my Yuletide Carol
I just want you to know
You're my Yuletide Carol
Do you really have to go?
You're my Yuletide Carol
Let's just stay under the mistletoe

Time goes by so very fast
If only I could make
Something so wonderful last
You're my Yuletide Carol
Do you really have to go?
You're my Yuletide Carol
And I love you so
Yes, you're my Yuletide Carol
And I, yes I, love you so

You're My Yuletide Carol
(Christmas Carol Version)
INTRODUCTION

Remember, the "reason" that Carol had come to Georgia, that December, was to witness the Christmas concert, and, certainly, for no other reason, such as to meet me.

So, in advance of the concert, Carol and I got together and shortened the original, to a "Christmas Carol" version of the song, which was performed on stage that following Saturday night.

I still envision Tony Bennett singing the Christmas Carol version of the song . . .

It just begs of being sung . . .

"And you're my yuletide Carol
And I love you so"

You're My Yuletide Carol
(Christmas Carol Version)

You're my Yuletide Carol
And I love you so
You're my Yuletide Carol
I just want you to know

Christmas bells are all ringing
And the skies are so clear
A warm fire is burning
As I hold you near

The light in your eyes sparkle
Like the new fallen snow
The nights are no more silent
You've got my heart all aglow

And you're my Yuletide Carol
And I love you so
You're my Yuletide Carol
Let's just stay
Under the mistletoe

In your arms, this Yuletide
Spirit I've found
Your love is enough
To last the year round

Time goes by so very, very fast
If only I could make something
So wonderful last

You're my Yuletide Carol
And I love you so
My hopes and my dreams
Won't be dashed through the snow

And you're my Yuletide Carol
And I love you so

You, Yes, You, Are There
INTRODUCTION

Hey! Guess what? Another love song!
This one is written to my first love, the first love of my life . . . And, still, the greatest love of my life . . . The Lord Jesus Christ.

In every way, He is the greatest.
He has always been there, by my side. He has never left me, even if everyone else did. He promised that He will never leave me, even until the end of the age. Guess what? The end of the age doesn't matter, because when that happens, I'll be with Him.

I have His Spirit dwelling inside of me, and He guides my mind, my heart, and my hand. Even though there were times I have left Him, He never left me. He protected me, and guided me, even when I didn't want anything to do with Him.
He always listened to me, even though I didn't want to hear from Him. He gave me gifts, and never took them away. When I returned, he renewed the gifts, made them even stronger, and added more gifts.

Even though I thought I could never love myself, He gave me a love for others.
He has been all, and is all.
I love Him.
The best part?
I am His!

You, Yes You, Are There

Day after day
Every step of the way
You, yes you, are there
Night after night
Dawn's early light
And you, yes you, are there

As I face today
Listening to what you say
I couldn't make it
Any other way

How much you care
How much you share
You, yes you, are always there
With you, I can face any day
And I wouldn't want it
Any other way

I am so glad
That I have you
And your love
To turn to

Every corner and every turn
Something new you reveal
You help me every step
Assuring me that you are real

Your strength is my strength
Your love is my love
I'm so glad you care
Your life is my life
I'm so glad that you, yes you, are there

I can't count on the weather
I can't count on me
Regardless the cost
It's you I want others to see

You are always with me
Replacing the shadows and doubt
I can now go help others
After you have helped me out

As long as you'll stay with me
Close by my side
I can rise above
Over the darkness, over the clouds
I can finish the race
Because I've already won your love

Skies may not be sunny
Raindrops may fall
Friends may not mean what they say
I know that you, yes, you
Will be with me every step of the way

So, bring on another day
Send another challenge my way
I know you'll be close
By my side you've promised to stay
And, I wouldn't have it
I couldn't make it
Any other way

Betrayal Confirms "It Took a Judas"

I only wish to encourage and comfort you, and I can do this best by sharing with you a little of my experience, but concentrating on the most important things: What I learned, what God taught me as I went through the process (and yes it is a process) of betrayal, recovery, and healing. Trust me when I say that what I thought was the worst thing to ever happen to me, and in fact was meant to destroy me and my ministry, turned out to be, in time, the best thing that ever happened to me. Of course, like you, I had no way of knowing this at the time . . .

You know all the emotions I felt, and none of them were good or healthy. But, and please listen very carefully: It was the way I handled the situation that turned everything out for the good. This is absolutely critical. The only thing you can do is to turn to Jesus, like never before, and trust Him, and Him alone, through the process. Do what He says, not what your family, friends, even selected members of the church family, etc., tell you to do. I don't mean to ignore Godly council. But, Godly council should not be something that will get you arrested, or someone seriously hurt (a church leader wanted me to join with him and a group and go "take care of the situation"). I realized, quickly, that I couldn't do anything in jail. I would be locked up, and those guilty would be free to continue their sin. Do what He tells you to do. Listen, and do. Believe, and follow through.

Pray, read your Bible. Then, pray, and read your Bible again.

Go to every church service you can. I was fortunate to live in an area where there were revival services, somewhere nearby, every night of the week. I went. I prayed. I read my Bible. I went to church. I prayed. I read my Bible. I then prayed again. If you are serious about recovery and healing, and knowing exactly what to do, and when, this is the only way. Pray, read your Bible, pray, read your Bible. It is true: Some things can't be beaten unless you pray and fast.

I can't overstate how, in the biggest crisis of my life, Jesus literally rushed to my side. "It Took a Judas," which I also call, "The Hymn of the

Betrayed," reads like a Psalm. Indeed, David struggled with being lonely, scared, angry, betrayed, and in despair. How often we read him crying out to God! It helped me to know that he felt the same way I did.

Someone asked me once how sharing a story of betrayal would glorify God. Well, the betrayal wasn't an end, only the beginning. Sometimes, the best thing that you can do to help someone who is facing a struggle, a crisis, is just to tell them, "I know . . . I've been there . . . I understand . . . the same thing happened to me . . . and God brought me out." Remember, one of the reasons God rescues you, brings you out, is so that you can go back and get others.

Here's what I learned:
For the first time in my life I understood Paul's writing that you are supposed to love your wife the way Christ loved the church.
I spent hours wailing, praying, crying out to God . . . I understood, for the first time, Jesus in the Garden of Gethsemane.
I would also, in the middle of soul-wrenching prayer, gain the full revelation of Jesus' words from the Cross: "Father, forgive them, for they know not what they do."
Early on, Jesus told me to "Stand up and become the warrior I made you. Gather the other warriors and pray." Within 24 hours, incredible things began to happen.
I fell in love with Jesus all over again. I turned to Him, which was exactly the opposite of what the enemy had planned. His intention was for the betrayal to destroy both my ministry, and me.

Like Paul, I had to "go to Arabia." Which I did. I prayed and fasted, solid, for 24 straight days. I ate nothing but God's Word.
I couldn't explain this, but God had me start by reading 1 and 2 Peter. I realized that Peter had had a bout with betrayal also.
Then, I read Isaiah. To this day, just turning to the book of Isaiah stirs something deep within my soul.

I learned two lessons from the life of Joseph, when Potifer's wife tried to lead Joseph into sin, and I thank Dr. David Jeremiah for giving me these two:

"When Joseph lost his coat, he demonstrated something that some of us never learn: It is better to lose your coat than to lose your character." And, "Circumstances don't change character. They reveal character."

I learned that Jesus will go and get you, as in "the lost sheep." But, he won't tie you up, throw you over his shoulder, and bring you back forcefully.
I realized that this betrayal wasn't the end. It was the beginning.
That, it's not what you lose . . . it's what you gain.
I learned that "A little sin never stays little."

For me, God showed me the story of Abraham, from Genesis. That I should go into a far land that He would show me, away from my father and my kindred.
For some time, I had this idea that I was going to have a son. And, when that happened, I was to name him "Daniel." That kept running through my mind for months before any of this happened. Daniel. Son. Son. Daniel.
I had no way of knowing that events were leading up to my moving away . . . far away . . . to a town called "Danielson."

My prayer is that this encourages you, and helps you in your struggle . . . right now.

When I was going through my battle, God put me in places where I would hear just the right word, or read just the right thing. My hope is in the Lord, who brought me out. The same Lord and Savior who will bring you out, if you will only let him. This hope is the reason I have shared this story, and my prayer is that I have written it, for you, for "such a time as this."

> And, always remember,
> *"When the pain is so deep*
> *And it hurts so bad*
> *And you just don't understand*
> *Just remember, My child,*
> *It took a Judas to fulfill God's plan"*

Grieving and "Acceptance" of Losing One's Child

I do understand that the hardest loss to accept is when a parent has to deal with the loss of their child. I have felt it, and witnessed others grieving the loss of a child. I also understand that the age of the child doesn't matter. Whether accident, or illness, or military casualty, to have one's child taken, by any means, is the most difficult tragedy of all to face. However, it seems so much harder to accept when it is an infant or young child, meaning also that the parents will be very young, and, often, this is the first real tragedy of their lives that they've had to face.

"Acceptance" was written as a result of the loss of an infant, who never left the hospital, except for being transferred to a children's hospital after being born. She never arrived home, where a nursery had been prepared by her two loving, expectant, and overjoyed parents.

The parents were young, and one of the most active members of our local church. Indeed, the father would become the Assistant Pastor just a few short years after. The father's family was one of the original founding members of the church, and his was the largest family in membership. His wife started attending the church long before they were married, and in fact, it was at this church that she had accepted Christ as Savior. Their courtship and marriage, followed by their Spirit-filled service to the Lord, was one of the great "stories/highlights" of the history of the church. Carol and I were honored to have been guests at their wedding.

It wasn't long before the first child came along. You know that the entire church family was as excited as they were. They had already "adopted" the baby as theirs, long before she was born. The pregnancy was normal, no complications at any time during pregnancy, birth, and afterward. She is a wonderful, beloved and adored, healthy child to this day.

A few months later, it was announced that the second child was on the way. And, once again, I think the church family was just as excited and expectant as the parents. The pregnancy went even smoother than the first, and joy and excitement built as each day moved one day closer to the birth of their second child.

I think we all remember where we were when we got the news that the young mother was in labor . . . then she was rushed to the hospital . . . we all waited . . . waited . . . waited . . . to hear the joyous news. However, the news we got shattered us to the core . . . the baby had been born . . . but something was terribly, dreadfully wrong.
Without going into details, the baby was born with underdeveloped major organs, including the heart. The baby was rushed to the children's hospital, and a very few, short days later, she passed away. Stunned . . . shattered . . . every emotion imaginable-and unimaginable. How do you comfort the parents? Perhaps the single sentence containing the most gut-wrenching emotion and passion, is only one word in length, and ends with a question mark:
"Why?"

What makes this sentence so emotionally charged is that it is being asked not only by the parents and family, but friends and relatives. And, let's face it. It is a question that, at times like these, even those acquaintances who aren't friends are thinking the same question. Those whom we have witnessed to, who may not have responded to our invitations or witness, will now, perhaps more than anyone else . . . be looking to see how we handle "this." I must say this, because it has to be said: It is exactly at times like these, when "the world is watching," when we must be the witness, the Christian, that we have, to them, claimed to be. However, what makes this situation so tough is that other true Christians, born-again believers, which, being human also, will have this same question. And, they too, will be closely, intently watching to see how you handle "this."

And, trust me, this only adds to the weight of the grief. For, now, you have not only the weight of the situation to bear, but you must bear the added burden of their doubt and fear. And, how you handle "this" may be the one witness that brings them to Christ, or draws those Christians experiencing this pain, closer to Him.

Our Pastor has made this statement, and I have used it myself on many occasions: There are some questions that we just will never get the answer to, on this side of Heaven. And then, when we get to Heaven, we won't have the question.

I do know that to effectively minister to others in great pain, we must have experienced great pain. And, as a minister, you will never look into the eyes of anyone who has not experienced great pain. It is how you have handled the greatest pain in your life that will be the most effective witness to others.

So, while grieving for their child, God gave me this poem. I wrote it, in one sitting, while sitting in my van, early one morning, in our driveway. I still have the memo pad sheets with the notes scribbled on them.

Almost always, God gives me the title for a poem before I write it, or at least during, or immediately after the poem is written. This poem was completely different, and this was the first time this had ever happened: I could not think of a title for the poem. For the first time, I had no clue; I was completely blank. I think it was because I was still in shock over the child's death, and, being human, it was so hard to deal with, and I knew all about the question, "Why?"

I struggled with the question of the title for several days. This had just not happened before. A few days later, Carol and I were staying on Cape Cod, a weekend getaway. I still hadn't come up with a title, even though I couldn't stop thinking about it.

I remember going to sleep watching the Christian channel. In the middle of the night, I was abruptly awakened . . . God spoke to me, clearly and plainly, and He only spoke one word: "Acceptance." I knew immediately what He meant.

This was the only time I had ever written a poem, in which the title was not included within the body of the work.

1 Peter 5:7: *"Casting all your care upon him; for he careth for you."*

It Was True: "Dear God I Just Don't Understand"

This is one of my works, born out of tragedy, which reminds me of some of the Psalms. Didn't David, at times, feel abandoned, all alone? How he cried out to God, in fear and desolation?

There was a time when I was truly all alone in the world. Or, at least I felt I was. I was the victim of a heart-wrenching betrayal, and was trying to piece my life back together. As a result of the betrayal, I was living all alone, in a new place. I did have a good job, working for various electric utility companies across the Southeast. I was traveling for at least five days or more out of the week. Often, I was in a different city every week, meaning a different hotel. I had suffered a serious ankle injury, and could not walk without the assistance of crutches, braces, etc. I still worked. I worked for a contract electric meter reading service, so I am probably the only person who ever read a route, in and out of the truck, all day, reading electric meters (and dodging dogs), on crutches.

I had always been athletic, and, as part of my job, I could run all day long. I was in great shape. It had been years (being pulled out of a crumpled car at sixteen) since I had suffered even a hint of an injury. Yet, here I was, feeling alone in the world, always in a new place, and I couldn't even walk. I honestly didn't know if I would ever be able to walk properly again, let alone run. I spent weeks doing the "physical therapy" stuff, and I finally got rid of the crutches. I could walk again, unassisted.

Shortly after I had recovered from the ankle injury, I was mixing work with ministry. It was early one morning, and I don't remember what town I was in. I was working a sub-division, and feeling great about working for the Lord "on the side." I didn't see him, but a big dog had hidden himself underneath a car, and as I passed by, he literally sneaked up behind me, and bit me on the right calf. This was the same leg which had the just-repaired ankle. After some choice words for the dog, I pulled off somewhere, cleaned, and then bandaged my right leg. Good job! Company protocol required that I go to the emergency room, file a report, and the rest. However, there was no one available to relieve me, so I kept on.

It was late afternoon when I was working a housing project just outside of town. As was the norm, I would move from one section to another, using back yards as a shortcut. I noticed several people had dogs, all tied up. As I approached the single-level apartment building, there was one dog, in particular, which was going nuts, standing up on his hind legs, straining every link of his chain. He was going ballistic, and I had a couple of choice words for him as I walked by. Suddenly, he broke the chain, and came at me. I fought him off, literally, but not before he had torn up my left leg, pretty badly. I found out the dog's name was Harley, as his owners ran out, and were beside themselves with concern . . . and worry about potential consequences.

Well, tough guy that I was, I left the housing project, pulled off, and did my best to bandage myself up. I tried to continue the route, but, and I'll be as kid-friendly as I can, it got to a point where I could not stop the bleeding, and I was really concerned that I was scaring people with my mangled leg. So, I went to the hospital for my first epidermal-type shot, the type that goes up your spine, and cripples you for a while.

I'll never forget being on the radio, as the entire utility crew heard me trying to get another supervisor to come out and finish the route. I like to think I gained their respect, however, as I radioed in that I was afraid I wouldn't be able to walk soon, and I couldn't get the bleeding to stop. That I should have enough strength left to make it to the hospital. You could just feel them listening, as a fellow supervisor radioed back, "I'd love to help you out, buddy, but I've got a safety meeting to go to." I eventually made it back to the hotel, where, I felt more alone than ever.

It was during one of these "alone" times that I was really questioning God. I never doubted God, at any time. He was just so faithful. But, I was suffering a string of "Why did this happen to me-itis" (I think that's a new medical term), and dear God, I just didn't understand. Alone, crippled again, deserted, you get the idea.

The physical pain I felt was nothing compared to the mental and spiritual pain I was going through. Of course, there were times I felt even more alone than at other times. Suffering a dog bite was a part of the job, and I used to joke that I had been in every emergency room in Georgia. And, a couple of other states. I have a long list of "emergency stories" involving accidents, near-accidents, and injuries, which maybe I'll share one day. On occasion, in public appearances, I will share a "dog story" or two, if it goes along with the message.

Something else happened on one of these road trips, which I have yet to share with anyone. I always carried my Bible with me, tucked away inside my suitcase. Yes, I would take it out when I got to the hotel! I used to carry my own microwave oven with me, before I started staying at hotels that had a microwave included with the room. I lived on TV dinners. Sometimes, I would carry equipment with me in the company truck I kept, so, often, I would have to put the suitcase in the back of the truck, while I was traveling to a new town. I would eventually get a locking toolbox for the truck. On one of my trips out of town, I had the suitcase in the back of the truck. Frankly, I had forgotten about it, as it was a weekday, and I had gone directly to the utility company, instead of checking in at the hotel first. Sometime later in the day, I remembered: The suitcase! I looked in the back, and you guessed it. Someone had stolen it. In stealing my suitcase, they had stolen my most important possession-my Bible! Imagine what I was going through, the natural doubts that came with my circumstances, and now . . . my Bible had been stolen. I just didn't understand.

Something else I have never written about. When I got home, I wasn't totally alone. My dog, "Baby," was my constant companion when I was at home, or when I went anywhere that wasn't work related. She rode with me, and hiked with me all over the mountains. I made sure she was taken care of when I was gone. I loved her so much, and she loved me. You know what I mean: We just had a way to communicate with each other, and she was, I thought, "all I had left," having raised her from a "baby," when she was small enough to sleep in her dog bowl. She was the daughter of Abraham (whose mate was Sarah), whom I wrote about in "Goodbye Abraham."

One Friday, I arrived back home, having been gone all week. Baby was gone. Someone had taken her, and I never found out anything further.

This was right in the middle of "all this," and of all the things I didn't understand, this moved quickly to the top of the list. I still miss her.

It was during one of these times of great discouragement and loneliness that, there in a hotel room, all alone, I reached for the hotel stationary, and put my feelings on paper. I really didn't understand, and I pleaded with God for the answers.

As I write this, I think about how this doesn't sound like someone who writes motivational and success articles. Yet, I am sharing this because we have all been there. Even Jesus has been there, and He never deserted or left me. He knows what it's like to be alone, to be betrayed, to have all his friends "run off." And, pain and suffering? How can I even mention what little I had been through? But, it is important to share this, as a way to encourage you. Even David, Israel's greatest king, went through these same feelings. And, he wrote about it. Reading that King David, and yes, even Jesus, the apostle Paul, and so many others went through these same things, just bolsters my faith. It means so much to me to know that they would understand.

As we find encouragement in their words, I pray you'll find encouragement in mine.

I think, deep down, that the real reason that we are so comforted by their writing, even in troubled and tragic times, is that we know how the story ends. David would become the greatest king. I say it often, because it is so true. What happened to me has happened to so many: I had no way of knowing, at the time, that what I considered to be the worst thing that had ever happened to me, turned out to be the best thing that ever happened to me. God's promises are so sure and true. The end is better than the beginning, and, the middle.

Now We Know "Why, Pastor, Why"

It was Sunday night, April 13, 1997, during the Sunday night service at my home church. From my perch inside the sound booth, I listened intently to yet another spirit-filled, power-filled message from my Pastor, "Pastor Dan."

As Pastor Dan delivered these sermons, entire congregations were constantly held in awe as the words seemed to flow from the very heart of God. Gazing down from the sound board, I heard Pastor Dan discuss the awesome grace and mercy of God, as the Pastor humbly shared how he did not know, nor could even understand, how God could reach down and save him from Hell, after all he had done in his life. Pastor Dan confessed that he did not even deserve to carry water into the sanctuary, to even be a water boy for the church! No, Pastor Dan could not understand why God loved him so much, and then to allow him to serve as Pastor, was even further beyond his comprehension.

Later that night, after returning home, I pondered Pastor Dan's questions about "Why?" Then, the Lord spoke to me, and told me "Why." Jesus answered the Pastor's questions, clearly writing them on my heart. The words came as fast as I could hastily scribble this direct revelation, onto a yellow legal pad, as I sat at the dining room table.

It took me 10-15 minutes to write "Why, Pastor, Why," as the words just flowed from my pen as fast as I could write.

I also realized, as I looked at the written words, that what God had revealed to me about my Pastor . . . the same statement should be able to be made about every Pastor, everywhere. If they truly are searching for the very heart of God, then we should also know, "Why, Pastor, Why."

So much has happened since I first wrote "Why, Pastor, Why." When I was given the poem, I didn't even have a typewriter; I had to borrow one from a church family. I didn't have a computer, so I had to make copies at the church.

After I wrote "Why, Pastor, Why," God made a very specific promise to me about the poem. And, not just about the reasons behind it. He made a very clear promise about my writing. His exact statement, without using the same words He used (which were so personal, I don't dare write them here), was that everything else would spring from this poem. Regardless of what else may happen, this poem must be first, and the rest would build as a result.

Of course . . . I tried other writing efforts . . . and each time, the door closed.

It was only when I released "Why, Pastor, Why" that things began to fall into place. I mention all this to make the point that God is faithful to His promises.

Allow me to also add: It is ok to remind God of His promises! It is not <u>Him</u> that will ever forget! You should remind God of His promises so that <u>You</u> won't forget!

And, I can relate so much to Pastor Dan's questions about "Why." Here's how:

How could God allow me . . . yes, me . . . to encourage and minister to Pastors?

God's grace, and mercy, is limitless.

I think of Paul, who was a real scholar, and it seemed he knew "everything about everything." He had been trained by the best. There seemed to be just one thing he could never quite figure out: "Why" Jesus chose him? If you read about the early life of Paul, you'll understand what I mean.

Jesus has got to have the most faith of anyone who ever lived! He chose a man who was lost . . . a man who did not even "know where he was" . . . to lead others out. He chose a man who was once lost on the road of life, to show others the way out. How great God is!

I am often asked where the quote about the "Office of Pastor" came from: God gave me this statement in July of 2008, as I was speaking in Barrie, Ontario, Canada. I believe it as strongly now, as I did when God shared it with me:

"The office of Pastor is the highest office in the land.
For, the people choose the president. God chooses the Pastor."

Later, when preparing to speak at a Christmas program, "here in the 'states," God gave me this:

"The greatest gift God gives the local church is their Pastor."

The Story of "Don't Weep For Me"

Here is part of the transcript from a special program I had the privilege of being part of, in February, 2003.

INTRODUCTION TO "DON'T WEEP FOR ME"

My intention for tonight is to offer a few words of comfort and encouragement to those in our church family who have suffered grief and sorrow as a result of losing loved ones recently.

Tonight, I'd like to share with you a poem that I wrote in honor of, and in memory of, my father-in-law, Mr. Vincent Martone. Many of you here knew Mr. Martone, as he attended church here the last months of his life, until he became too ill to get out, and then finally had to have "around the clock" care at a nursing home.

I'll never forget the first time that he came to church here; it was a Sunday morning. Mr. Martone had 3 sayings that I will always fondly remember him for, and he used them all that morning. As I was helping him along, down the sidewalk, up the steps, and into the building, taking it easy, one step at a time, he reminded me, "Inch by inch, everything's a cinch." This has already become something that I catch myself saying today.

It became time to meet the Pastor. As the Pastor and Mr. Martone exchanged greetings, introducing themselves, Mr. Martone quipped, as only he could, "Do you get paid by the job or by the hour?" As they parted, Mr. Martone then told the Pastor a saying that he was most famous for . . . whether he saw you at the store, at a restaurant, maybe you were the mailman, or a doctor. Whether you saw him often, or this was the first meeting, he would always end the conversation with, "Remember that God loves you and so do I!"

I'd like to add that I loved Mr. Martone, and always loved just being around him, watching and listening to him. I once heard Paul Harvey say, "The most important thing that a man can do for his children, is to love their mother." There is another saying that I would like to add:

"The most important thing that a man can do for his father-in-law, is to love his daughter."

I've said before, and it comes to me again, that I believe that we need more men who are not afraid to stand up and say, "I love Jesus," "I love my wife," and "I love my family."

There is something now that I would like to say, publicly, about Carol: Carol did everything she could for her father. Her whole life seems to be one big sacrifice. She spends almost her entire existence doing things to help other people. Like many of us, especially when we first become members of God's family, Carol would wonder, "What's *my* gift?" The apostle Peter described Jesus this way in Acts 10:38: "How God anointed Jesus of Nazareth with the Holy Ghost and with power: who went about doing good . . . for God was with Him." Again, to repeat, Carol's entire life is spent doing things for, and helping other people. That puts her in pretty special company, and let me add that she may have "the greatest gift of all."

During the previous months, Carol tried to do all she could for her father . . . the long drives . . . the sleepless nights . . . going days without a decent meal . . . just watching his condition worsen, and, at the same time, still helping others all she could. She had never, not one time, complained. Let me allow that to sink in before I take a small part of it back: The only time she ever got disgruntled, or upset, or complained was this: She would feel so bad, even cry, because she felt like she had not done enough-that there was more that she could or should do.

Part of my message tonight is not just to her, but to all who have experienced that same emotion. Sometimes, for reasons we will never know or understand, there is just nothing more that we, or anyone else, can do. It's just not in our hands anymore. It's funny, but just by sharing this with you, a small part of what she has done and gone through, it strikes me that she has helped even more people . . . those of you, here tonight . . . Now, that's a gift!

There is something else that I would like to add, for those of you who are still mourning the loss of a loved one. I hope that this, in some small way, helps. My younger sister, Susan, who was the most bubbly, faithful person I have ever known, contracted cancer at age thirty-four. The family found out in the summer, and by early September, she was gone. She had beaten cancer once before as a child, and part of my early childhood experiences was going to St. Jude Children's Research Hospital, in Memphis, TN, where she was a patient.

We were all so sure that she was going to be healed this time. After she died, I had real trouble understanding, and accepting the fact that cancer had killed her. The biggest question was "Why?" Then, in the middle of the night, I was awakened from a sound sleep. As I stared at the ceiling, wondering what noise had caused me to awake so abruptly, God spoke directly to my heart, in a voice just like I am speaking here to you. God spoke only nine words, but it was all I needed. In a voice "plain as day," He said, "What happened with Susan is between Susan and me." The peace of God overwhelmed me, and I never questioned Him again.

The very first official act that Carol and I did as husband and wife, upon leaving Ringgold, GA (where Susan had also gotten married), was driving to the cemetery in Tunnel Hill, GA, where, together, we placed the bridal bouquet on Susan's grave. Of course, it was Carol's idea. I fully expect Susan to be one of the first ones to greet Carol in Heaven. It will be the first time that they will ever meet.

It was just after 4:20 on the afternoon of November 4th, one day after Carol's birthday, when I received the call from Carol, letting me know that her father had just passed away. I told Carol to stay right there, to not go anywhere. I left work, and fought the tears as I drove the 57 miles home. As I entered the house, and just held Carol tightly, I'll never forget the very first words she spoke. She said, through the tears, "They weren't upset because you had to leave early, were they?" I just about lost it right there! I was heartbroken that even now, all she could think about was me. I did not say it, but I thought, "Man, Carol . . . Sweetheart . . . just once . . . just once, think about yourself."

Soon, we arrived at Mr. and Mrs. Martone's house, meeting the rest of the immediate family to discuss arrangements for the funeral service. Mrs. Martone looked at me, and asked if I would read something at the service. I told her it would be an honor. A few minutes later, Mrs. Martone looked at Carol and asked, "Carol, do you know what he will be reading?" Carol looked at her mom, and gave me the biggest compliment I've ever received. She said, "He'll know. He'll just know what he's supposed to read. God will give it to him." Yes, my first thought was something about she must know something I don't!

What kept running through my mind was that I needed to write something that Mr. Martone would want to say if he was here. Over and over, all I got was the phrase, "Don't weep for me, don't weep for me." I thought it odd that it was "don't weep," not "don't cry." Later that night, in my home office, I tried to concentrate on doing other things. As is usually the case, God will give me a line here and a line there, as the night goes on. Every 15 minutes or so, I would get another line, turn away from the computer, and as fast as I could write, I put the lines down, and then return to work. Somewhere around 2:30 in the morning, I had all the lines, and "Don't Weep for Me" was done. I knew it was complete.

The obituary came out in the paper in a couple of days, which detailed Mr. Martone's military service. I had forgotten about this part of his life, so I went back in and wrote a new section about his overseas service, and then felt like I needed to include the line he was most famous for, so I added that.

After I wrote "Don't Weep for Me," I realized that it was not meant to just comfort Mr. Martone's family, but for all families, everywhere, during their time of loss. My prayer is that this really will bring comfort and peace to your souls, this day . . ."

The Wrong Restaurant Leads to "The Sweetest Sound I've Ever Heard"

I was new to Connecticut. I only knew how to get to work in Hartford, to our church, and to the Salvation Army Thrift Store (they had a great collection of albums). I was to meet Carol and her mother, Rosalie, at a restaurant in Danielson, for a nice dinner, after work. The restaurant was their favorite, and I knew exactly where it was, as I passed it every day going back and forth to work. I assured Carol of this; not to worry, I go by it every day, and I knew exactly where it was. I mean, how many restaurants do I pass, in a small town, where the name is the first name of the owner? No problem. Did I need to write down directions? No way!

So, I stopped in at Hank's, a very nice local restaurant, and since I had gotten there first, I picked the best spot in the house, right by the fireplace. The fire was bright and cheery. The perfect spot! I sat for a while, and after quiet a while, I was still alone. They must be running late, so I ordered a big plate of ribs, and they'd catch up when they arrived. I eat slowly anyway, so this seemed ok. More time passed, and I started getting uncomfortable about being alone, at a big table, the best seat in the house, as groups of guests came in, glaring at me and my ribs, alone at a banquet table, as they squeezed into booths.

It never once dawned on me, at any time, as the night wore on, that I may have come to the wrong restaurant. I was busy thinking about how blessed I was, and how much God had blessed me with Carol and our life together. And, thinking about how God had brought us together, for both of our futures. Only a few days before, Carol had accepted Jesus as her Savior, giving her life over to Him. It had happened at home, just me and her, and it happened right in the center of our kitchen. Even though we have moved, I can still see the exact location on the floor, see us holding hands, praying together, Carol asking Jesus to forgive her, thanking Him for giving His life for her, for helping and healing her, then thanking Him for His forgiveness, accepting Jesus, right there, as her Lord and Savior.

Only a few months before, I had proposed to Carol, just before she flew back home to Connecticut, in the center of my kitchen, back in Georgia. I thought about how God had changed everything in our lives. How big a change in Carol's life Jesus had already made. To this day, Carol continues to be the most influential Christian influence in my life.

But, that night, everything was still new, and I just basked in God's love, as I sat, alone, by the roaring fire. I thought about how it happened, how awesome God was, and I was so proud to have played a part in leading Carol to salvation.

We had made a promise to each other that we would read the Bible, together, every night, before going to sleep. It just made sense to start at the beginning, as Carol had never really read the Bible before, so we started reading in Genesis. I would read a little, and then she would read a little. She would ask me questions along the way. Genesis can be a tough book for seasoned Christians to understand, and, right from Adam and Eve, she had plenty of questions. The poem is really self-explanatory as to what happened next.

It only took 14 chapters for Carol to realize what she had to do. Someone, a dear Christian, asked Carol, years later, what she was currently reading. She responded, "The Old Testament." Their response was, "Why are you reading that?" The answer to why the Old Testament is so important is included in the poem.

By sharing this, I am also sharing the fact that Carol wasn't a Christian when we married. She was, and still is, the most genuinely nice person I have ever met. But, that doesn't get you into Heaven. It is only through the Way, the Lord Jesus Christ, the only way to the Father, that your salvation is secured, and assured. I know this raises the question of "being unequally yoked."

Carol and I met through mutual friends in Georgia, Ed and Lucille. Ed, one of the finest Christian men I have ever known, asked me this question, after Carol and I started planning our wedding. Was it right to marry Carol, a non-believer, with me being a believer? I can only answer this by telling you my situation and circumstances. With Carol, I just knew. I knew it was the right thing to do, and that it was God's will and plan. I just knew. I proposed to Carol only three days after I had met her. I had a great job, traveled all over, had a company vehicle, expense account, the works. And, I was working with good friends. I gave all this up, to sell most of my possessions, and move over 1,000 miles away. To a state I had never set foot in.

I just knew it was the right thing to do. I never doubted. I can't stress enough how important it is how you face difficult situations, especially tragic circumstances. The world, yes those you have witnessed to, and other Christians, will all be watching how you handle a bad situation. Not a single person, who really knew me, doubted that it was the right thing to do. Not a one. Why? Because they had seen me go through the worst possible situation, and saw how I handled it. Granted, it wasn't me, but God working through me, which "did it." But, understand, it was how my actions witnessed to them, which they based their opinion on. I did seek Godly council. One Pastor, who knew me personally, in fact, worked with me, quoted Philippians 1:12, where Paul wrote that all the bad things which had happened to him, was "for the furtherance of the gospel."

One of the most blessed compliments I have ever received was when we called my friend Ed, back in Georgia, to let him know that Carol had just given her heart to the Lord, had accepted Christ. I'll never forget his response: "Well, I knew it wouldn't be long."

It was a little over a month.

Oh . . . back to the restaurant . . . I was thinking about all this, how so much had happened in such a short time. We even had a great church home with a wonderful Pastor and wife. Then, God gave me this great idea for a poem, to praise Him, to thank Him for Carol's salvation, and all He had done. The words burned inside me, just as the logs in the fireplace were illuminating the faces of those in the room, which were huddled in their booths, staring at me, and all of the empty chairs at my table. Of course, I was busy eating, and I didn't have any paper. I didn't dare bother the waitress. I had been trouble enough tying up the best table in the place, alone. I wasn't about to ask for anything else.

I did have a pen in my shirt pocket, but no paper. What to use? The only thing available was a napkin. Since I was eating ribs, and more guests had been expected at my table, there were lots of napkins. I started writing on a napkin, but that didn't work. Maybe napkins only work for business plans? Anyway, what now? I had to make a van run. I hurriedly darted outside, but, of course, no paper in the van. This was before I made sure to always have a memo pad in the van. The only paper of any kind I had was in the trash bag. The grocery list from last week. Yes! This might work! I quickly hurried back in, anxious to get this written.

Ignoring the stares as I sat back down, I went to work. On the left side of the paper were the grocery items, with lines marked through. This gave me the right side of the paper to write. On the back of the list, left side, my figures were written, as I had added up the grocery total, item by item. This gave me room on the right side there, as well. So there, at Hank's, alone, on the grocery list I had dug out of the trash from the van, I wrote, "The Sweetest Sound I've Ever Heard . . . The sound of my wife reading God's Word." Now, years later, I am looking at that grocery list, marveling at the prices . . .

And, continuing to marvel at the grace God continues to show toward myself, and Carol.

Oh, by the way, who would have known that a town so small would have TWO restaurants with the owner's first names? As I proudly left Hank's, poem in hand, full of ribs and thinking how proud Carol would be of me . . . I drove through downtown, where I passed George's Galley on the left . . . where Carol and her mom had enjoyed a fine dinner, even though frantic over where I was . . .

Writing "I Stopped by Your Place for Christmas" at the Cemetery

It was just a few days before Christmas. It was Saturday, and Carol was at work. A big storm was moving in. I wanted to be sure to go to the cemetery before the snow came, to "tidy up" the gravesite of my in-laws, Carol's parents, Rosalie and Vincent Martone.

Carol and I made regular visits to Westfield Cemetery, making sure the gravesite was properly groomed, to water the flowers . . . Carol made sure to place a special wreath on the center headstone with each changing of the season . . . and to just visit. We missed them so much, and now, when the winter snow came, the ground, and yes, their graves, would be covered with snow for several months. It had been a good winter thus far, meaning that here it was, days before Christmas, and there was no snow. But, we both knew that would change soon. If we were going to do any work at the cemetery, today, Saturday, may be our last chance before spring.

Upon arriving, I parked, as always, under the big maple tree on the side of the dirt road which led from the center of the cemetery to just to the right side of their resting place. I spent a few minutes just visiting, talking to them both. It was especially sad today, because it was just before Christmas, which was their favorite time of the year. They loved the whole Christmas season, but especially the times spent with close family. Today was Saturday. We would have had the big family Christmas party at their house . . . tonight. And, they would have been at our home on Christmas Eve, just a couple of days away.

After spending a few minutes visiting, and let's face it, mostly thinking about how much I miss them, how much it just doesn't seem like Christmas anymore without them, just thinking . . . I got jolted with a new idea for a poem . . . It just encompassed my entire being . . . it was something I had to write, and I had to write . . . right now . . . right here.

Right!
Right here in the middle of the cemetery, I was going to write a poem.
Right!

Those of you who write, know exactly how and what I felt. I had to grab a paper and pen and jot down notes. But, this was different from the usual "wake up in the middle of the night, and grab a pen" scenario. It was the same feeling I get when God gives me something specific to write . . . I have to write it down, and I have to write it down now. And, fast. I don't know how many times I've come running in from working in the yard, with a "get out of my way!!!" mentality, racing into the office to grab a pen and paper, having to write down a new revelation which God has just given me. I've written on bird feed bags, cardboard scraps, etc., being afraid I would lose the thought before I made it back into the house.

The words, "I stopped by your place for Christmas, the place where you always stay" kept racing through my mind, and I had to get this written down right now, right here!
I raced to the van . . . my trusty pen was there, where it always was, in the heater/air conditioner vent. Now, I reached for the note pad I always kept on the dashboard . . . but it wasn't there! I frantically searched the van, under the seats, in the glove box, but I had no paper! Where was the note pad I always kept in the van??? It wasn't there! I tore through the glove box. The only paper, of any kind I could find, was a bank deposit envelope. Being ever frugal, I kept one on hand, so that I wouldn't have to use a new one from the bank each time I made a deposit.

I had no choice. The bank deposit envelope had bank advertising all over it. There wasn't enough room to put my initials between the sentences. So, I tore open the bank deposit envelope, making a single sheet, of sorts, on the inside. Fortunately, they weren't frugal enough to realize the inside is blank, and would make a great place to advertise their interest rates.

Now, I had my pen, and paper. But, where to write? I had no clip board, or anything in the van to place behind the paper, to support the paper as I wrote (the bank was frugal enough to buy cheap paper).

So, I stepped out of the van, and placed myself in front of the center of the hood of the van, using the hood of the van as a writing desk, and right there, right then, under the maple tree, just a few feet from their graves, I wrote the words as they came.

I remember, clearly, the teardrops falling on the paper, as I wrote the words . . .

I stopped by your place
The place where you always stay

Heroes . . . the Alamo . . . and Jesus

A few years ago, Carol and I had the opportunity to visit San Antonio, Texas. San Antonio is an awesome city, and we had a great time. We had the opportunity to visit all the tourist attractions. We loved the Riverwalk, Hemisfair Park, where they had held the World's Fair, the Alamodome, and of course, the Alamo. Now, what does that have to do with Jesus? Well, we took Jesus with us. It's ok to take Jesus with you on vacation, you know.

A couple of notes about flags: When you fly the United States flag, and you fly another flag beside it, the other flag has to always be flown lower than the United States flag. That is, except for one flag. I didn't know this, but there is only one flag that is allowed to fly at the same height as the U.S. flag. And, that's the Texas flag. The reason why is because Texas declared its independence as a Republic in 1836.

While we were there, we went to the NCAA Women's Championship game at the Alamodome. Before the game, they have the pre-game ceremonies, and the national anthem. Before the national anthem was sung, they brought out the torn, ragged flag that had flown over the World Trade Center. You could feel the chills that went through the crowd. I'll never forget that moment. It was then that I realized the sacrifice that those men and women, the firefighters and policemen, made that day back in September, 2001. And, here I was, five blocks from the Alamo, and I wondered how many of those men and women that went back inside the Twin Towers knew that they were not going to come out, and they still went back in. I thought about heroes. Real heroes. Not the guys that sit on the bench and make five million. Real heroes, willing to give their lives for others. And then, you know what? Suddenly, my job didn't seem so bad after all.

The Alamo. It is the most famous mission in the world. I believe that the Alamo is probably the second most recognized building in the United States, next to maybe the White House or U.S. Capital. Something I didn't know: The Alamo doesn't receive any state or federal funding. It is all donations. It is guarded day and night by fully armed Texas rangers.

When you visit a museum, and it's getting near closing time, a friendly voice comes out and says, "Ladies and gentleman, our museum will be closing in fifteen minutes. Please begin making your way to the exits. Thank you." Well, the Alamo closes at 5:00 PM, and at 4:59, armed Texas rangers appear, and they shout, "Ladies and gentleman. The Alamo is now closed. You'll have to leave NOW!!!"

It had been a life-long dream of mine to visit the Alamo. Growing up in Georgia, I would read the stories, and since Tennessee was next door, Davy Crockett and his volunteers were every boy's heroes. And, Jim Bowie. And, William Barret Travis. And, the rest. Plus, my birthday is March 6th, which is the same day the Alamo fell, so I've always felt a bond there.

It occurred to me that I had never seen a picture of the inside of the Alamo. The reason why is, that no pictures are allowed to be taken inside. Think about it: Have you ever seen a picture from inside the Alamo? There is also a sign asking men to remove their hats. This is because the Alamo is a shrine. A memorial to the 189 heroes who fought impossible odds and died there.

Behind that famous wall is a long corridor which is lined on both sides with plaques honoring those who died, and there is a flag for each state, or country, that is represented. I had no idea how many men from other countries died at the Alamo. England. Scotland. France. There were four men from Georgia who died there, and there was one man from Connecticut, a man named Jennings, who died at the Alamo.

As we were walking by this line of flags, we kept looking for the Connecticut flag. We went all the way down one side, and were about three quarters of the way down the other side of flags, when we came to the Georgia flag. I looked at Carol, and she was thinking the same thing. You don't suppose? Right after I moved to Connecticut, the state quarters came out. Georgia was third, then the Connecticut quarter came out, fourth. I thought that this was confirmation that I was meant to be there. So, as we looked at the Georgia flag, I looked at Carol, and said, "You don't suppose . . ." And sure enough, at the Alamo, standing right next to the Georgia flag, is the Connecticut flag. You could feel the chills.

We all know the story of what happened. I'd like to share just one story. William Travis, the commander at the Alamo, had sent messengers to get help, but no help came. He realized it was his men, only 190, vs. approximately 7,000. He called all his men together, and told them that help was not coming. Those who stayed, knew they would die. Then, he took his sword out, and drew a line in the sand. By the way, this is where the phrase "you've crossed the line" and "draw a line in the sand" comes from. He then asked those who would join him to fight for freedom and liberty, and to fight to the death, to cross the line.

I thought that this is what Jesus is doing now. He's drawing a line and asking, "Who will join me?" It's interesting that in this scenario, His side is life, and the other side represents death. Sin and death. So, he is asking who is willing to give up their life and follow Him. You have to choose one side or the other. You can't straddle the line. The problem is, that so many go to his side, and then go back over to the other side. Or, think they can keep jumping from side to side.

When William Travis drew that line in the sand, every man, but one, crossed that line to join him. Jim Bowie was deathly ill, and had already given his command over to Travis. Jim Bowie was there on a stretcher, and asked his men to carry him over the line. I thought that's the same decision we have to make. Sometimes we're sick, or tired, or "sick and tired," or fed up with the way the world is treating us, but we still have to make that decision. To stay true to the line we have crossed. Stay true to Jesus.

The one man who did not cross that line was from Jim Bowie's group. His reason, and I'm quoting as historically accurate as possible, his reason for not crossing the line was "I'm not ready to die." That's another statement that has everything to do with Jesus. But, listen to this. It was Jim Bowie who stretched out his hand, over the line, to shake hands with this man, and wish him well. I thought that is just like Jesus. Even after we make the decision to not cross the line, to not follow Jesus, after we've decided to pursue a life of sin . . . Jesus is still there, His hand over the line, still reaching out to us, and He would be the first one to welcome us back.

While in San Antonio, we stayed at the Menger Hotel (somehow that sounds like a pitch from a game show), which is the oldest operating hotel west of the Mississippi. It opened some fifteen years after the battle of the Alamo, and so many famous people, from presidents to writers to actors, have stayed there. Teddy Roosevelt recruited his Rough Riders there. It was incredibly nice, and late one night I was filming and taking pictures inside the lobby, when a man that worked there told me I might just get a picture of a ghost, as this is one of those old, historic places that have a reputation for ghost sightings. I looked at him and just said, "The only ghost I believe in is Holy . . ."

The hotel is located right next to the Alamo. I mean you walk out the door, and it is sidewalk, street, sidewalk, the Alamo. The last night there was Monday night, and that night I had a dream. Right next to the Alamo, any idea what I dreamed about? Jesus.

I dreamed that I was there on the morning that Jesus was crucified. But there was one huge difference. I dreamed that I was Jesus. God allowed me to see just a glimpse of what He went through for me. Now, I'm not saying that I knew everything Jesus did, or felt exactly the way He did. But the beatings and whippings were happening to me. And, I felt no anger. It was like "this is what I came here to do." I caught just a glimpse of what Jesus felt. His love for all mankind, willing to give His life for everyone else. Even those who were killing Him.

In my dream, I was taken to be beaten and whipped twice, and without going into too much detail, it was bloody. I don't know if you've ever had a dream where something happens to you that should be really painful, but in the dream, you don't feel any pain. That's the way this was. I never yelled or screamed. I just accepted what was happening to me as just something that I had to do. But then, they laid down the crossbeam, and got me ready to have the nails driven into my hands . . . Well, that's when I freaked out. That's when I panicked. Just the thought of those nails going into my hands was too horrible, too painful to take. That's when I stopped being Jesus, and became me. I woke up in a cold sweat, too terrified to scream. And then, I started to think. Think about heroes.

The apostle Paul . . . and, by the way, the apostle Paul had his head cut off, but he never crossed back over that line. Paul said that, sure, a man would, maybe, give his life for a just or righteous man, or would die for a cause, a country, or his family. But think about what Jesus did. He died for sinners, for people who hated Him, for the people who killed Him. And, He died for you and me.

Jesus has to be the bravest, most courageous man who ever lived. Think about this: Every minute of every day, every day of His life on earth, He knew how He was going to die. And, not just die. But, the way that He would die. I think of a boy growing up in San Antonio, walking by the Alamodome, and thinking to himself, "One day, I'm going to play there. One day I'm going to play for the Spurs or some other team, and I'm going to play right there in the Alamodome. All eyes are going to be on me."

Now, in Jesus' time, crucifixions were something that you saw all the time. Can you imagine, when Jesus was growing up, eight . . . nine . . . ten . . . twenty . . . thirty years old, and He saw someone being crucified, what in the world would He be thinking of? Every day of His life, He knew this was going to happen to Him. He still went through with it.

I know that I couldn't have done it. Like most guys, I think I'm macho, or too strong to cry, or show pain. I work hurt, sick, tired-I always answer the bell. I don't remember having a sick day for years. Once, I tore my lateral collateral in my right knee. I worked right through it. In order to walk, I would have someone actually take a hot iron, and literally, iron my leg. When I was reading meters, I got attacked by dogs two times in one day. The first time was at about 8:30 in the morning, and once I got the bleeding stopped, I climbed back into the truck and kept going. I got attacked again at about 3:30, and I kept going, but I had to stop because I couldn't stop the bleeding, and my leg was so gruesome to look at, I thought I might scare people.

Later, I would tear ligaments in my right ankle, while suffering a second degree sprain. I wore a special ankle cast, and I really thought that I'd never be able to run again. But, using crutches, I was able to walk, and I didn't miss a day of work. I read meters on crutches, and drove a straight shift truck.

What I am trying to say is that I always thought I was tough. How many of you guys have ever said this about another guy, usually someone in sports, "I've got more guts in my little finger than they have in their whole body!" Well, I'm here to tell you now that Jesus Christ had more courage, in just one molecule, that I'll ever have in my entire life. Pilate said it right when he said, *"Behold the man!"*

One of the best sermons I ever heard was by a preacher who was preaching at the Douglas County Jail in Douglasville, GA. He told an audience of 200 inmates, "You think you're big and bad? I'm here to tell you right now that Jesus is a baaaad man . . ." He knew his audience would understand . . .

He then went on to tell of things that Jesus did, and could do. We think of men like boxers and guys like that, who are supposed to be big and bad, but this same preacher said to look at the guys that King David hung out with if you want to see bad . . . the men that could kill, in battle, hundreds of men by themselves. So, I'm here to say that the greatest hero of all time is Jesus Christ.

Now, the message I have to deliver is that we should not take for granted what those brave men did at the Alamo. We should not take for granted what those firemen and policemen did in New York City, and most of all, we should never take for granted what Jesus did for us, either.

John Newton: Who Am I?

For several years, I had researched the life story and history of John Newton, the author of "Amazing Grace." One of my favorite historical characters to portray on stage is John Newton, which I do in full period costume, always with a local talent to sing the verses of the song, at points within the presentation.

Since we have included the new "Amazing Grace: The Jesus Amendments" as part of this volume, as well as sharing all of the known verses to the song, I felt it was appropriate to include this brief biography of John Newton. It was written in a "Who Am I?" format, to go along with the script of my "Amazing Grace: The John Newton Story" stage portrayal. His story is . . . well . . . amazing!

I was born in 1725, and I died in 1807.

The only godly influence in my life, as far back as I can remember, was my mother, whom I had for only seven years. When she left my life through death, I was virtually an orphan.

My father remarried, sent me to a strict military school, where the severity of discipline almost broke my back. I couldn't stand it any longer, and I left in rebellion at the age of ten. One year later, deciding that I would never enter formal education again, I became a seaman apprentice, hoping somehow to step into my father's trade and learn at least the ability to skillfully navigate a ship. And I determined that I would sin to my fill without restraint, now that the righteous lamp of my life had gone out. I did that all the days in the military service, and I further rebelled.

My spirit would not break, and I became increasingly more and more a rebel. Because of a number of things that I disagreed with in the military, I finally deserted, only to be captured like a common criminal and beaten publicly several times. After enduring the punishment, I again fled. I entertained thoughts of suicide on my way to Africa. I decided on Africa, because it would be the place I could get farthest from anyone that knew me. And again I made a pact with the devil to live for him.

Somehow, through a process of events, I got in touch with a Portuguese slave trader, and I lived in his home. His wife, who was brimming with hostility, took a lot out on me. She beat me, and I ate like a dog on the floor of the home. If I refused to do that, she would whip me with a lash. I fled penniless, owning only the clothes on my back, to the shoreline of Africa, where I built a fire, hoping to attract a ship that was passing by. The skipper thought that I had gold or slaves or ivory to sell and was surprised that I was a skilled navigator. And, it was there that I lived for a long period of time.

I went through all sorts of narrow escapes with death only a hairbreadth away, on a number of occasions. One time, I opened some crates of rum and got everybody on the crew drunk. The skipper, incensed with my actions, beat me, threw me down below, and I lived on stale bread and sour vegetables for an unendurable amount of time. He brought me above to beat me again, and I fell overboard. Because I couldn't swim, he harpooned me to get me back on the ship. And, I lived with the scar in my side, big enough for me to put my fist into, until the day of my death. On board, I was inflamed with fever and enraged with the humiliation.

A storm broke out, and I wound up again in the hold of the ship, down among the pumps. There, bruised, confused, bleeding, and diseased, I was the epitome of the degenerate man. I remembered the words of my mother.

I cried out to God, the only way I knew, calling upon His grace and His mercy to deliver me, and upon His Son to save me. The only glimmer of light I could find was in a crack in the floor above me, and I looked up to it and screamed for help. God heard me.

Thirty-one years passed. I married a childhood sweetheart. I entered the ministry. In every place that I served, rooms had to be added to the building to handle the crowds that came to hear the gospel that was presented, and the story of God's grace in my life.

My tombstone reads, *"Born 1725, died 1807. A clerk, once an infidel and libertine, a servant of slaves in Africa, was by the rich mercy of our Lord and Savior, Jesus Christ, preserved, restored, pardoned, and appointed to preach the faith he once long labored to destroy."*
I decided before my death to put my life's story in verse. And that verse has become a hymn.

My name? John Newton.
The hymn? "Amazing Grace."

Letter to Mama

Written from Berlin, NH, to Rocky Face, GA: November 7, 2010:

Hi Momma:

We always used to joke that being late is a family trait . . . here is the package I was telling you about. I am sending you a book that was used as part of a Children's Literature class I am taking. As soon as I read it, I had to send it . . . after you read it, you'll know why.

Sometimes, 1,000 miles away really does seem like 1,000 miles away.

We pray for you often, and continue to be amazed, and so grateful, for the glaringly obvious fact that God has His hands upon you. And, will continue to do so.

I know that God loves you even more than I do, and He is with you, at your side, always, and at every step.

I mentioned the 1,000 miles. During this process of healing that you are going through, I have never, ever, seemed so far away. My comfort lies in the same Source as yours: That even though I can't be there . . . God can, and is.

I know that often, healing is a process, always longer than we want, and even more often, healing is painful. However, it seems that we are never more in the palm of His hand, than during the healing process. Yet, these are the very times that we sometimes feel that He isn't there at all. This reminds me of the "Footprints" poem. I know He will continue to hold you there, in the palm of His hand. Now, and always.

It is Sunday night here, and it is 33 degrees. In a month (or less), that will seem like a heat wave.

Mama, I always think, and I always remember what you've said about the changing seasons. That it proves, once again, that God is in control.

I think so often of so many things you've said. And, done. In fact, I am reading through Psalms again . . . and am at Psalm 119. I never read the Psalms, or even hear or think of a verse from Psalms, that I don't immediately think of you. I am trying now to think of a verse that I could quote . . . but there are so many that fit, how do you pick one? There are so many. I am at Psalm 119: 41-48. I think that, instead of quoting one for the current situation, I should quote one that you would want me to live by, to illustrate the living witness that you have been to me, and for multitudes of people. One that would make you happy to see demonstrated in me: I just read Psalm 119:35: "Make me to go in the path of thy commandments; for therein do I delight." I know that nothing brings you more joy than to know that "thy children walk in truth."

Carol is leading a ladies Bible study at church, and many lives are being changed. Even now, Carol is writing to a girl we sponsor in Tanzania, Africa. Our business has allowed us to minister to, and bless people all over, and yet, we are just beginning. We will continue to answer the Call that was made so long ago.

Will close for now.

Know that this writing brings with it all of my love . . . and gratitude . . . for the most wonderful Mother who ever lived. And, we will continue to pray for you, and Daddy, and for all.

Personal Thoughts on Pastor Appreciation

Pastors: We have so many reasons to bless them, and do all we can to help them:

Their dedication, their support, their devotion, their love, their sacrifice, and their leadership.

I use the word "their" because they never act alone, yet they are alone so much. They feel alone, because they are human. I know . . . isn't it amazing that we actually feel strange admitting that Pastors are human? After all, we expect them to be super-human. And, in many ways, they are: They are super, and they are human. Let's face it: We feel that way because we expect them-yes, expect Pastors to do things that we either couldn't do, wouldn't do, or don't think we can do. Or, to put it more bluntly, things we are afraid to do. We forget that they are called to do exactly the same thing we are: To do all we can for the Lord. Are we? Do we? We expect them to. One of the Pastors I most admire told me, "People don't understand, and would not believe, just how discouraged Pastors get." We must take every opportunity to express our dedication, our support, our devotion, our love, for their sacrifice and leadership.

I heard this from a Pastor, at a memorial service, in his effort to comfort those who were mourning: "Jesus understands how you feel. He knows what it's like to be sad, to mourn, to hurt, to be hungry, to be cold, to be alone." By understanding how Jesus felt, we can understand how Pastors feel.

It's interesting that we could add the word "to" to each phrase: Their dedication to God, their support to God, their devotion to God, their love to God, their sacrifice to God, their leadership to the church on His behalf. And, what they do for Jesus and His Gospel, they do for us: Their dedication to us, their support to us, their devotion to us, their love to us, their sacrifice to us, and their leadership to us.

We could also add the word "of" to each phrase: Their dedication of, their support of, their devotion of, their love of, their sacrifice of, and their leadership of. They are a living example of Jesus, doing all these things for us, just as Jesus did all for us, on our behalf.

It is always "their" because the Pastor is always the under-shepherd, Jesus' representative as Shepherd. We are His sheep, His Flock. Jesus commanded Peter to "Feed my sheep," not "your sheep." The Pastor never, ever forgets just whose sheep he is watching.

My prayer is that, as we remember their calling as Pastor, we also remember our calling. Only then, can we truly understand what the Pastor goes through each day . . . not just on our behalf . . . but on His behalf.

I must close by adding this, because I have to: People are always asking me, asking each other . . . asking everyone except the Pastor . . . "What is the most important thing I can do for my Pastor?"

I know, they mean well, and usually, yes, their heart is in the right place. I am always asked for my answer to this question. First, I believe the most important thing you can do for a Pastor is to be faithful to pray for them. Pray for your Pastor, your Pastor's family, and your Pastor's ministry. Because, trust me, all three are constantly under attack. Allow me to repeat that: Pray for your Pastor, your Pastor's family, and your Pastor's ministry. Because, all three are constantly under attack. Did I mention that all three are constantly under attack? They are, so please pray for all three.

Next, the most important thing you can do for your Pastor is be faithful to their calling, and faithful to their ministry. This means go to services, and help your Pastor-yes volunteer in any way you can. Be faithful in attending your church services. Money, gifts? No, the best way to support your Pastor, in a physical sense, is to be faithful to attend services. And, yes, this means special services.

Do all you can to show that you are "with" your Pastor in every way; that you are on the same page as your Pastor. Show that you believe in what your Pastor is trying to say, and trying to do. Be faithful.

There is one common thread that runs throughout: The word, "faithful."

The first sentence of my answer began with the phrase, "The most important thing you can do for your Pastor is to be faithful . . ."

This is absolutely true, and every Pastor would agree. The most important thing you can do for your Pastor is to be faithful. Faithful to Jesus . . . faithful to your calling . . . faithful to do exactly the same thing which you admire the most about your Pastor: To do all we are called to do for the Lord. To be Jesus to those whom we meet. To be like Jesus in every area in our lives. To be completely devoted to Jesus, to express Jesus in our hearts, our minds, and our actions.

To fulfill the words to the poem, *"When I look at you, it's Jesus that I see."*

I believe that every Pastor would agree that what they want from us the most is what Jesus wants from us the most. Our lives, in service to Him. Which is just what we envision the Pastor to be. I have news for you: This is just what our Pastor envisions us to be.

Yes, it is a popular phrase, "What would Jesus do?" I believe every Pastor would agree that the important question is, "What would Jesus want me to do?"
Let's do all we can to bless our Pastor, our Pastor's family, and our Pastor's ministry.
The greatest gift God gives the local church is their Pastor.
Let's not wait until a special day, or week, or month. Let's bless our Pastor and our Pastor's family, in every way we can, as often as we can.

Presenting "Why, Pastor, Why" to Pastor for First Time

People often ask me what I would say as part of a Pastor Appreciation Day Service.

I found a page of notes I had taken to make a presentation to my Pastor, on Pastor Appreciation Day, several years ago. This was the first time the words of "Why, Pastor, Why" were ever engraved onto a plaque, and this was long before we took the poem and launched the website, "Pastor Appreciation Gifts."

I share this with you so that perhaps you may glean some words to share with your Pastor. I also include part of a story I shared with the congregation, which I hope you will enjoy:

"For Pastor Appreciation Day, we all want you to know how wonderful and special a man you are, and how blessed we are that you are the man God chose to be our Pastor. You've touched all our lives in so many ways, and we want you to know how deeply we love and honor you and appreciate the sacrifices you've made for us.

We all have stories of how you've made a difference in our lives, and I'd like to share just one example:

Just this last April, on a Tuesday night, April 27th . . . we had just started coming to church here . . . It was only the previous Saturday, April 24th, that Carol had accepted Jesus as her Savior . . . in the center of our kitchen . . . the Pastor and his wife came to visit us that next Tuesday night, and as always, with me being from Georgia and Carol being from Connecticut, the question is always asked about how we met. I explained that, after talking with Carol for months on the telephone (mutual friends had arranged our initial phone call), I had never met her. When she finally came to Georgia, I went to Atlanta Hartsfield Airport, with friends, to greet her for the first time.

I had told Carol, as we planned our first-ever meeting at the airport, that "I would be there with bells on." When I arrived, sure enough, I was wearing "jingle bells" (one of those bell-straps they hang on business doors) underneath my jacket. Keep in mind that this was squarely in the middle of the holiday season, and Carol's only reason for flying the 1,000 miles from Connecticut, was to meet me . . . I mean . . . to attend the annual Christmas concert which our mutual friends always performed at a local venue. What happened at the airport, as I figuratively "strutted" across Atlanta-Hartsfield Airport, my solid metal bells safely concealed underneath my jacket, I have never written about, and only a handful of people know. So, I share it here for the first time:

This was in December, 1998. Remember? Earlier this day, the United States had officially gone to war, and had begun dropping bombs on Bagdad. I remember the audio clips, on the radio, as I sped toward Atlanta, of President Clinton addressing the nation, informing us that we were at war. My head was swimming as I readied myself over my first meeting with Carol, and having increased airport security as a result of our war in Iraq just didn't figure into my planning.

(NOTE: Remember this was "pre-9-11," so increased airport security was just not something we planned for . . . and, let's be honest . . . before 9-11, we never figured "security" as part of our plan, for either flying, or just picking someone up at the gate . . . we never added time to our schedule for security reasons . . . this was before we "lost our innocence.")

I was making my way to the gate to meet Carol, when I was confronted with the security gate/walk through. Where you had to empty your pockets, and walk through the "portal." To put it mildly, the alarms went off . . . really loud. On me. Really loud. Loud enough so that everyone in the airport could hear, and then look at me. Have you ever had that "Look, y'all, I'm innocent" face?

I was asked, as I completed my walk through the portal, to stop, and "step to the right." I did this, as it seemed the entire airport stopped . . . no motion . . . all eyes looking at me . . . as the airport security guard raised that "scan" bar, ready to do a full body scan, in front of, literally, God and everybody. I'll never forget the look on the guard's face, as he began the scan at my head, then toward my chest . . . as the bar lowered to my chest . . . the alarm on the bar went off . . . really loud . . . I already had the airport's attention, and now, I had the attention of the "associate guards," who swarmed around me . . . as the alarm continued to sound . . . There was no doubt . . . and, you could tell from their faces . . . that I was carrying concealed metal underneath my jacket . . . The airport security guard, nervously, right hand holding high that scan bar; the other hand, nervously reaching inside my jacket . . . nervously, as the crowd gasped . . . waiting . . . he reached in . . . felt what must have set off the alarm . . . grasped it . . . and, as if in a fishing contest, raised the jingle bells high from out of my jacket's confines . . . and held, bravely it seemed . . . my jingle bells . . . high aloft, for all to see . . .

I was just caught up in the moment of looking at all of the weapons which the associate guards had holstered on their sides, and at their right hands, which were all, tensely, on top of these holsters, as if waiting to draw. I was the only target within distance.

I don't know which look I remember most: The look when the alarm first went off, or the look on the airport security guard's face as he raised a set of "jingle bells" high above his head.

I told this story to the Pastor and his wife, and I am sure I told a much longer story than he had expected. However, at the end of the story, he was still awake, and attentive.

I also mentioned that, as Carol had just gotten saved just 3 days earlier, I wanted to get her a new Bible, but couldn't afford a nice one like I wanted to give her.

Anyway, we had a nice visit with the Pastor and his wife, and told them we would be there for Wednesday night service, which just happened to be the next night. The last thing the Pastor said was, "Great . . . I'll be there with bells on."

We walked into the church on Wednesday night, and two remarkable things happened. The Pastor was standing in front of the church, and when he saw us enter, I'll never forget the look on his face.

But, it was what he did next that amazed me, and showed the type of man he really is. Of course, he was wearing a suit . . . he reached under his jacket . . . and, attached on a string . . . was a set of jingle bells!!! He exclaimed, "See, with bells on!" Then, he and his wife walked up, greeted us . . . and presented Carol with a brand new Bible.

They had just been to our home, less than 24 hours before . . . And, how many times, I wonder, at the close of a visitation, had they heard, "Yeah . . . we'll be there . . . next service . . ."

2 years ago, in Georgia, God gave me "Why, Pastor, Why" for Pastors all over the world. But, as I stand here this morning, I'm not so sure that this was not given to me, just for you . . . In closing, as glad as I am that I moved to this city, I am just as blessed that you decided to move to this city."

September 11 Anniversary Memorial Speech Transcript

I'd like to share with you part of a speech I gave during a memorial service to commemorate the anniversary of 9-11. This is the edited transcript:

"I'm going to share a few thoughts about Patriotism. First, it's ok to love your country. It's ok to love the United States of America. Yes, love God first-remember, it's always been "God and country." This nation was founded on Godly principles, by men who readily admitted they were trying to do, and stay within, God's will. I can even remember learning in school that the reason the Pilgrims first came to this country-first and foremost-was for religious freedom.

I believe that the greatest wave of patriotism in our lifetimes, and certainly since World War II, occurred after 9-11 . . . Being from the South, I've always said that "if they ever attacked even New Jersey, we'd be the first to get in line to fight." Well, they just about did. Those weren't just airplanes; they were guided missiles that were aimed to kill Americans.

It seems that after 9-11, there was such a huge wave of patriotism that extended everywhere, and I don't know if the feelings are as strong now. There is always the initial "honeymoon" type period, and then over time, as we get back to our jobs, and the pressures of everyday life, that maybe we lose some of the enthusiasm that we had before. But let me make one thing clear:
Ladies and Gentlemen, we are . . . still . . . at war. American men and women are still serving-and dying-overseas. American military personnel are stationed around the globe, and we all read the newspaper, or hear the news every day. For these American-and allied forces- the war is just as real now, as the first day.

I believe that each one of us, every morning, should hit our knees, and yes, thank God for salvation, but also thank God for the fact that He allows us to live in The United States of America. Most of us have no idea how blessed we are just to be alive in this country. Just to be able to come to a place like this-in public-and worship God. Just to be free. Just to be free.

Why does there have to be war? Well, consider this: As born again Christians, full of the Holy Ghost, Paul said it best when he described a war that we all have . . . inside ourselves. This is a war, a real battle for our lives, our souls, and it's raging inside us every day. How then, can we expect a lost world to behave toward each other?

Let me share just one story about "the world out there." First, estimates I've read show that there were more people killed for their faith-as martyrs- in the last century, as in all the previous centuries combined.

A couple of months ago, I attended a conference hosted by the Connecticut Anti-Slavery Group. Their purpose is to fight against slavery world-wide. I thought what some of you may be thinking: Why do we need such a group? After all, slavery was abolished. Slavery *was* abolished . . . but . . . only here . . .

Here's a statistic that is staggering: In the world today, there are 27 million . . . that's million with an "m" . . . 27 million men, women, and children, who are slaves. They are tortured, abused, and killed. The guest speakers were a husband and wife ministry team from just outside Boston. I describe them both as a modern-day Moses, as they have been able to free thousands of slaves from captivity. As they described the treatment of slaves, the entire auditorium was filled with gasps of "Jesus" and "Oh my God!" In these countries, a cow is worth 100.00. You can buy a cow for 100.00. A man, woman, or child is worth . . . 60.00 . . . A cow is worth almost double what a human being is. What this couple does is raise money, purchase slaves through the black market, and then release them. I thought about Christians dealing with the black market; then I remembered how many Bibles have been distributed through the black market.

Now, I'm going to give you a metaphor with The United States and the world. Us as Christians and the world, and then Jesus and the world:

Jesus is the light of the world, the hope of the world. The United States is a beacon of light, of hope, to the entire world. You have heard this many times since 9-11.

We as Christians are that beacon of light, of hope, to our individual world. Our family, friends, and people we work with, etc.

Why do people hate the United States so much? As you know, just try to stand up for what is right, try to live right, always try to say and do the right thing, be "different," and you'll have enemies soon enough-family, friends, people you work with . . . even an entire country.

Let me explain with scripture:

In Luke 6:7, Jesus healed the man's withered hand, in the synagogue on the Sabbath. The crowd watched him closely. Whether it was Jesus, then, or someone today, trying to be like Jesus, they will be watched closely. When Jesus had healed the man, Luke 6:11 says, "they were filled with madness/rage and discussed with each other what they might do to Jesus." The word "madness" here means "irrational fury." Think back on our lives, and think about how we acted while we were in sin. How irrationally we acted.

Never forget that our freedom came by a great price.

Our Christian freedom/liberty came with the greatest price of all.

I went to Ground Zero for the first time on July 12th. It is hard to describe the atmosphere. You look at the faces, and see tears, and expressions that seem to say, "I don't know how to act." The area is surrounded by fence, and the "big hole" does not exist anymore. There is a concrete floor, and you can see the beginning of construction. The one image that stays with you is the cross in the center. It is a large steel crossbeam, in the shape of a cross, standing all alone. I have been told that when they cleared the debris, at the very bottom of the pile, there was this steel cross, just standing there, beneath hundreds of tons of death and destruction. They decided to leave the cross there, where it had landed on 9-11.

I tried to ask the vendors, who were selling "Picture Books" of 9-11, and found it somehow disconcerting that no one I asked knew the story behind the Cross. I will never forget leaving Ground Zero, and 45 minutes later, I was safe inside Madison Square Garden, listening to the National Anthem.

Now, I'd like to again share with you a new Patriotic Poem/Song for America, "The Eagle Still Flies (Under Star-Spangled Skies)." When I wrote the poem, my intention was for it to become a new song, a new "Anthem" for America, to uplift and encourage not just us here on American soil, but for those men and women fighting overseas. Honestly, at the time, I did not think that the war would last this long. I feel like that is even more reason for this poem to go out."
Speech Delivered 8/31/03

The Eagle Still Flies: Mail Call

During the course of my writing and performing career, I have had the honor and privilege to correspond with so many people around the world. I have been truly blessed to have been given such a wide and varied audience for my writing. The greatest blessing, however, is the fact that I was the one directly given the words to these works. More often than not, I just "did what I was told," or just "wrote what I was told." That's why I don't like to take credit for the writing, because, as Carol so often reminds me, "Who wrote it?" My answer is always the same, because it has to be; it's true: "God wrote it. I just handled the pen. I was just the pen man."

With "The Eagle Still Flies," the audience was, as with all of my writing, for everyone around the world. As John Kennedy said, *"We all breathe the same air."* The message is for everyone. We all have the same feelings, heartbreak, and joy. And, we all have the same Lord and Savior. Who died for us all, and wants us to spend eternity with Him. How often I have been confronted with someone who was prejudiced, and I would have to remind them that "Jesus died for them, too!"

"The Eagle Still Flies" was a special situation for me, and I really felt led to personally send the work to specific individuals. Which, I did. By sharing portions of the letters, which I included with a copy of the work, I hope to give you further insight into how I felt about the work, and that it was specifically meant for a particular time and place. I have written and received many letters concerning this new "Anthem for America," and I wanted to share a sample of those here.

I have removed the strictly personal parts of the correspondence:

Excerpts of Letter to Joseph Daniels
President/CEO
World Trade Center Memorial Foundation

"It is due to my appreciation, and support of your efforts in relation to the building of the Memorial, that I am writing . . .

The very definition of "cause" leads me to particularly wish to share this work with you:

"A principle or idea that people believe in and work for."

It is this idea, this principle and what it represents for all Americans, not just as a structure or physical entity, from which the cry to be built emanates. The events of September 11, 2001, while local in execution, were national in intention. To build this Memorial, it will take the combined efforts of all Americans, for all Americans were deeply affected by the events which it will commemorate. It will take the efforts of a nation that is not joined *because of* the event, but a nation that was joined *before* the event. A nation that was, and continues to be, joined . . . united. For, the Memorial represents something that comes about not as a result of an event, but as a manifestation of something that was already in existence before the event.

Yes, we must build the Memorial. To "build" means "to make something by joining parts." How very appropriate that this Memorial will serve to commemorate, to remind, to honor, and to celebrate, all that this nation represents-before, during, and after the events of September 11, 2001. It will serve to continue to commemorate, remind, honor, and celebrate the true heroes and hope of America-who came to the forefront before that day, on that day, and on each day thereafter. It is only through the combined efforts of all Americans that this vision will be, as it should be, achieved.

I close with two quotes which I have posted on my office walls: "Although the world is full of suffering, it is also full of the overcoming of it" (Helen Keller); and, "It's not whether you get knocked down, but whether you get back up" (Vince Lombardi). I personally found most poignant, within your mission statement, the words, "courage . . . compassion . . . endurance . . . resolve . . . eternal beacons . . . freedom."

I would be amiss if I did not share one of my own: "I don't write about tragedy, or loss . . . I write about comfort, victory, and great gain."

We are proud of you, and will continue to support your efforts."

We all remember where we were, when we first heard the news. Like so many, I was at work, on a Tuesday morning, in September. Here's the first word I got, from an email.

From:
To:

Subject: IN THE NEWS

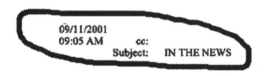

09/11/2001
09:05 AM   cc:
                Subject: IN THE NEWS

A TWO ENGINE PLANE JUST FLEW INTO THE WORLD TRADE CENTER IN N.Y. CITY AND THE BUILDING IS ON FIRE, HEAVY DAMAGE TO THE BUILDING. UNKNOWN WHY............ WAS JUST WATCHING THE NEWS, AND A JET HAS NOW HIT THE SECOND WOULD TRADE CENTER AND IS ON FIRE!

Just like so many of you, I had friends and business associates in New York City that day. Living in Connecticut, on a line between Boston and New York City, I have often wondered if those planes flew directly over my house ... For years, every time I would see a jet fly directly overhead ...

Excerpts of Letter to Mayor Michael Bloomberg

"I am writing in recognition of, and in appreciation of, your capacity as both Mayor of New York City, and as Chairman of the World Trade Center Memorial Foundation.

I admire your inspirational leadership shown during your tenure as Mayor. If demonstration is a question of ability, then, "you have answered well." I am especially proud of the great strides your administration has taken to improve the educational system, with proven results, within the city schools. Your achievements toward the advancement and improvement of the quality of education are certainly noted, and appreciated.

Carol and I have had the privilege of visiting New York City many times, and we cherish our time there among our most prized memories. Perhaps even more lingering than the "sights of the city" is the way we have always been treated by the people there-especially law enforcement. In all our travels, we have never been more welcomed or courteously treated, than by those in your city, who so genuinely and sincerely offered their help or services to us.

Thus far, I have only shared this work with President Bush, who was both gracious and supportive, and will be presenting a copy to Mr. Giuliani. My intent is to personally present the poem to a few select leaders, who, like yourself, have a particular closeness to the subject matter, and offer it in appreciation of their efforts and involvement in what "The Eagle Still Flies" represents.

The poem is very personal to me, as I believe it is for all Americans. For, I love New York. And, I love America. I can't envision one without the other. I look at your city as a microcosm of America, and when the attacks came, the target was not as much a city as a country. The city, like the country, is not comprised of boroughs, but brothers. And, how special is a city, to all who love freedom and the liberty it represents, that was deemed worthy to be presented a Statue of Liberty-from another country across the sea. I applaud your efforts in raising the Memorial, and join all Americans in the cause, knowing that it will take a national labor to give birth to such a noble child.

We will continue to lift you, your family, and organization, up in prayer. We are proud of you, and will continue to support your efforts."

THE CITY OF NEW YORK
OFFICE OF THE MAYOR
NEW YORK, N. Y. 10007

December 3, 2008

  I was honored to receive your poem. On behalf of the City of New York, thank you for your compassion and concern for those affected by the events of September 11, 2001. The outpouring of support we have received from around the world has been a tremendous source of comfort for us all.

  Again, many thanks for your kindness and best wishes.

      Sincerely,

      Michael R. Bloomberg
      Mayor

MRB:lt

Excepts of Letter to President George W. Bush

". . . I send my continued prayers and best wishes for you, your family, and your administration . . . It has not just been your courage, your leadership, and your example that we as Americans are so proud of. It has been your faith. Faith in God, faith in America, faith in its people. When I think of great Presidents, I think of those who were known to be men of prayer. I believe, Mr. President, that you are in great company. John Adams said, "There is no national security but in the nation's humble acknowledged dependence upon God."

I dedicate this anthem not only to you, but also to the men and women who are proudly serving America in the Armed Services. I offer this to bring hope, comfort, and pride to all Americans. Everywhere. It also carries with it the starkest of reminders, that the war is just as real now, as the first day. For, the cause is just as real today. And, tomorrow.

I wish to tell both them, and you, that thanks to your combined efforts, the eagle does fly, under star spangled skies.

I close with this quote from Daniel Webster: "God grants liberty only to those who love it, and are always ready to defend it."

Carol and I will continue to lift you, your family, and administration, up in prayer."

THE WHITE HOUSE

WASHINGTON

March 30, 2005

Thank you for taking the time to write and for your kind words.

I am humbled and honored to lead a proud Nation. Through courage, compassion, and strength, Americans are demonstrating the character of our country.

Our Nation faces great tasks, and we are meeting them with courage and resolve. My Administration is committed to continuing our economic progress, defending our freedom, and upholding our deepest values of family and faith.

Laura and I send our best wishes. May God bless you, and may God continue to bless America.

Sincerely,

George W. Bush